Study Skills for Business and Management Students

Other titles in the series

Scullion and Guest, *Study Skills for Nursing and Midwifery Students*
Latto and Latto, *Study Skills for Psychology Students*

Study Skills for Business and Management

Students

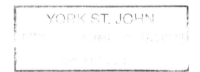

Barbara Allan

 Open University Press

Open University Press
McGraw-Hill Education
McGraw-Hill House
Shoppenhangers Road
Maidenhead
Berkshire
England
SL6 2QL

email: enquiries@openup.co.uk
world wide web: www.openup.co.uk

and Two Penn Plaza, New York, NY 10121-2289, USA

First published 2009

A catalogue record of this book is available from the British Library

ISBN: 0-335-22854-2 (pb)   ISBN: 0-335-22853-4 (hb)
ISBN13: 978-0-335-22854-6 (pb)   ISBN13: 978-0-335-22853-9 (hb)

Library of Congress Cataloguing-in-Publication Data
CIP data applied for

Typeset by RefineCatch Limited, Bungay, Suffolk
Printed and bound by CPI Group (UK) Ltd, Croydon, CR0 4YY

Fictitious names of companies, products, people, characters and/or data that may
be used herein (in case studies or in examples) are not intended to represent any
real individual, company, product or event.

The *McGraw·Hill* Companies

Contents

Series editor's preface

Study skills include all the abilities that make it possible to cope with the demands of academic and professional pursuits. For people just embarking on a course of study these skills include being able to deal with all the intellectual, emotional and social challenges that are part of the day to day demands of being a student. Beyond the skills involved in coping are those that enable students to do really well in their chosen disciplines. These include much more than the ability to memorize or understand the topics of study, spanning issues relating to time management, ethics and the personal and interpersonal upheavals that often have such an important impact on the student's life.

The study skills that are mastered at university or, for some people earlier when studying at school, are central to what everyone has to offer as a graduate and/or professional. Some people would even suggest that the main contribution of a university degree is to provide a person with the skills for studying. It is these skills that will help the person through the rest of their career.

Studying is a skill that can be mastered like many others, by first understanding the process and then by developing appropriate habits through active involvement. Yet while there are some aspects of the process that are common to all forms of study there are often important facets of any particular area of study that demand special skills. Further, even when the skills may be relevant across a number of different disciplines it is usually easier to understand what is required by embedding consideration of them within the specific topic.

The Study Skills series is therefore being published to provide guidance on how to be an effective student within each of a series of specific domains. By dealing with study skills in relation to an area of study it is possible to ensure that the examples are directly pertinent to the student of that area, rather than being general exhortations. The books thus complements the many other publications available on more general topics such as essay writing or taking examinations.

The focus on particular areas of study also enables authors to follow a particular educational trajectory from the early entry into college or university right through to becoming a recognized professional in that chosen discipline. It allows the authors to draw on examples that speak directly to students about issues in their own lives. It also enables the books to identify particular topics that are of special significance for any given discipline.

This series therefore provides a valuable resource to all students, which they can draw on as a friend and guide throughout their course of study and beyond.

David Canter
Series Editor
University of Liverpool

Acknowledgements

The starting point for this book was the University of Hull Business School's *Study Skills Handbook*, which I wrote and have edited for the past five years. Thank you to all students and colleagues who contributed to this work. In particular, I would like to thank colleagues in the Study Advice Services at the University of Hull who provided me with valuable feedback on what helps and hinders students' learning. Chapter 9 draws on the work of Anthea Gregory, Val Monaghan and Gabriele Vosseberg, who generously provided me with copies of their module handbooks for the Professional Experience Placement year and also the Study Abroad year, which helped to inform the content of the chapter. I would like to thank them for their knowledge and expertise in these specialist areas.

Special thanks must go to all the students who have attended my sessions on study skills, emailed me or visited my office with interesting queries about academic practices and professional development. It is these business and management students who have guided my personal development.

Finally, I would like to acknowledge and thank my husband, Denis, and daughter, Sarah, for their support and patience throughout this project.

1

Introduction

Introduction • Getting started on your degree programme • What do you study on a business or management degree? • Ethics and professionalism • Subjects not covered in this book • Topics covered in this book • Summary

Introduction

This chapter provides an introduction to the book and it will help you to orientate yourself and become familiar with the ideas and approaches to studying required for being successful in a business or management degree. The book is written as a general reference guide and I suggest that you read this chapter and then skim through the rest of the book. You can then choose when to read individual chapters in greater depth. You may read and work through individual chapters in any order. This means that you will be able to relate your reading to the academic demands of your programme of study.

The aim of this book is to provide you with guidance on the academic skills needed for success on your business or management programme of study. By developing these skills, you will also become the type of employee that many organizations are actively seeking. Feedback from employers suggests that they are seeking employees who are able to:

- Work independently and as part of a team
- Communicate effectively in writing, in meetings and in presentations
- Find and use different types of information
- Work to specific briefs
- Use basic project management skills
- Manage themselves and their workload

- Work in an ethical and professional manner
- Continuously learn and improve their performance.

As a result of reading and working through the topics in this book, you should be able to:

- Improve your personal management skills
- Prepare yourself for becoming a success in the workplace
- Understand the different approaches to learning and teaching used on your programme
- Find and use business and management information
- Understand and prepare for different assessment methods
- Successfully plan and complete an extended project, dissertation or independent study
- Work in groups
- Plan and take part in a professional experience and study abroad
- Prepare yourself for moving into the world of work.

Getting started on your degree programme

You may be reading this book in preparation for going to university or college to study for a business or management degree. Alternatively, you may be reading it at the early stages of your course or as you become aware that you need to develop your study skills. At the start of your degree programme you will find that you need to spend time getting to know the university or college, your department or business school, and your programme of study. You will be invited to attend induction and enrolment events, and you will probably find that there is a lot to learn. Settling into your degree programme is explored in Chapter 2.

It is important to realize that in studying for a degree, you are engaging in a learning and social process that will change you and your future life. The more active you are in this process then the more you will benefit from it. In these days of student fees, there is often talk about 'students as customers', but universities and colleges are not supermarkets selling particular products. Instead, they are educational organizations that provide and facilitate structured learning experiences, and they provide a wide range of resources such as people, libraries, computing centres and study advice services that support students in their endeavours. This means that students who engage with the learning experience and make full use of the resources and facilities are more likely to do well and obtain a *better* quality qualification than those who think university is an extension of school. One of the important roles of universities is to accredit your learning achievements via assessment activities so that you leave with a credible degree, diploma or certificate.

Students on business and management degree programmes come from an extremely wide range of backgrounds and countries. This includes individuals who are:

- School leavers and studying in their home country
- School leavers who have travelled to another country to study
- Part way through their degree programme and are taking part in an exchange or study abroad experience
- Returning to study after a gap year or other break
- Studying a programme in a second language
- Topping up a qualification, e.g., a foundation degree or diploma gained in a college
- Changing career and returning to study after many years in the workplace.

This means that you are likely to be in a group of extremely diverse people with very different previous educational experiences. This is one of the real benefits of studying for a business or management qualification: you will learn to study and work in diverse teams. You will also gain an international group of friends.

What do you study on a business or management degree?

Students studying business and management cover a wide range of topics. The actual topics will vary depending on the specific degree programme and also the research interests of your business school or department. In the UK, the Quality Assurance Agency (see www.qaa.ac.uk) provides what are known as 'benchmark statements' and these help to set the standards of business and management education. Your degree programme is likely to cover a wide range of subjects and these include the following:

- Accounting and finance
- External environment including economics, politics, environmental, ethical, legal, political, sociological and technological factors
- Information systems, and information and communications technologies
- Management and organizational behaviour

- Management of resources and operations
- Markets and marketing
- Organizations and their structure, culture, functions and processes
- Strategic management.

You will also explore generic themes such as sustainability, globalization, corporate social responsibility, diversity, business innovation, creativity, enterprise development, knowledge management and risk management.

Some degree programmes offer a 'common first year' in which all business and management student cover a wide range of topics and they may then specialize in the later stages of their course. Typical topics in a common first year include:

- Introduction to accounting and finance
- External business environment
- Introduction to communications and information technologies
- Introduction to marketing
- Management and organizational behaviour.

These topics provide students with a basic understanding of key aspects of businesses and organizations. There will then be opportunities to specialize and follow up topics of interest and also courses that enable you to gain professional accreditation.

Business and management programmes are designed to enable students to develop a wide range of skills including:

- Ability to reflect and learn from experience
- Critical thinking skills
- Decision making skills
- Effective communication skills
- Effective learning skills
- Effective self-management skills
- Effective use of communication and information technologies
- Information skills
- Interpersonal skills
- Leadership skills
- Numeracy and quantitative skills
- Problem solving skills
- Project management skills
- Research skills
- Team working skills, including the ability to work in diverse teams.

These skills are likely to be taught through the main subjects included on the programme, for example team working skills may be taught as part of a management and organisational behaviour module. In addition, you may be able to develop your skills through specialist skills courses and also through a wide range of additional activities (see Chapter 3).

Ethics and professionalism

When you enrol on a business or management degree you are taking the first steps in a professional career and one that is grounded in the real world. As with vocational courses such as medicine or law, you are joining a professional course and, at the end of this course, your future employers will expect you to behave in a professional manner. Many business schools and departments introduce the idea of ethics and professionalism at the very start of the course and this theme is embedded in the whole programme. It may be covered in specialist modules or units within the course. In addition, students will be expected to behave in a professional manner by being on time for scheduled events; sending apologies if you are going to be absent or late for an event, showing respect for others; and dressing in an appropriate manner. In addition, all students are expected not to use unfair means, for example cheating or plagiarism, in their assessed work (see Chapters 5 and 6). Some business schools have codes of conduct or professional principles, and employers who want to attract recruits who understand the importance of professional practice welcome the opportunity to recruit graduates who have a sound understanding of the importance of ethical and professional practice. In addition, professional bodies such as the British Institute of Management and the Chartered Institute for Personal and Development have codes of practice and ethical guidelines, and you may find it helpful to join a relevant professional body as a student member or when you obtain your first professional role.

Subjects *not* covered in this book

Business and management education is an extremely broad field and there are some topics that are beyond the scope of this book. These include quantitative methods and also information and communications technology.

All business and management students require basic skills in quantitative methods and these skills range from manipulating simple equations to reading and interpreting graphs. In addition, students need to be able to handle basic statistics. Some students will need more advanced quantitative methods skills, for example the ability to deal with time series analysis or calculus. The majority of business and management degree programmes provide both basic and advanced courses on quantitative methods and statistics. In addition, many universities provide special support or study services that will help you to get to grips with numerical techniques.

If you find quantitative methods challenging then my advice is to take advantage of the introductory courses that will be available to you as part of your degree programme. In addition, many universities and colleges run special workshops on topics such as 'confidence in maths' or 'becoming equipped in dealing with numbers'. Some students try to avoid quantitative methods and anything to do with numbers *but* this is an essential skill for working in business or management, and the absence of these skills will severely limit your career.

Case study

Mike was enrolled in a BA Management degree and had not studied mathematics since he had achieved a C grade in his GCSE five years before. He was shocked to discover that he was expected to study quantitative methods as part of both an Academic and Professional Skills module and also a Research Methods module on his degree. He would also need to be able to use basic numeracy skills for his first year Accounting and Finance module. Mike was so upset by this news that he considered leaving his degree and finding one where he wouldn't have to use numbers. He visited his programme leader, Jean, and she explained that nowadays it was very rare to find professional employment where you would not need to use numerical skills. She suggested that Mike visited the Maths Help Desk in Student Services, as they were very experienced in supporting students like Mike. Mike visited the Maths Help Desk and they asked him to complete a diagnostic test. Using the results from this test, they then advised him to sign up for some numeracy workshops. Mike attended eight one-hour workshops. Initially he was very apprehensive about going to these workshops. However, he found that they were led by a very friendly tutor and each workshop was limited to 12 students. Mike quickly found that he was making progress with his maths. He discovered that learning to use numbers at university was very different to his school experiences of maths and that he could do it. By the end of the workshops, Mike was feeling much more confident about the quantitative methods aspects of his course. When he began using quantitative methods in his degree programme, he discovered that he could manage it very well. He also saw that he was doing much better than many of the other students. He sometimes found that he needed to visit the Maths Help Desk for additional support, but they were always very welcoming and willing to help him. At the end of the first year, Mike obtained a mark of 61% in his quantitative methods exam and he was extremely pleased that he had tackled this issue rather than run away from it.

The majority of students starting a business and management programme have basic information technology (IT) skills, for example they can use a word processing package, search the Internet and carry out basic functions such as saving or copying a file on their computer. Students sometimes overestimate their IT skills and don't appreciate that they need to develop advanced skills in the following types of packages:

- Word processing, e.g., Word
- Database, e.g., Access
- Spreadsheets, e.g., Excel
- Presentations, e.g., PowerPoint
- Email systems, e.g., Outlook
- Bibliographic or reference management systems, e.g., EndNote or RefWorks
- Project management systems, e.g., MS Project
- Web 2.0 tools, e.g., weblogs, wiki.

You may find that there are opportunities to develop your IT skills as part of your degree programme or as an enhancement activity. Some universities and colleges provide optional courses that enable students (and staff) to develop their IT skills and gain additional qualifications, for example the ECDL (European Computing Driving License).

The ability to deal with numbers and IT will help to make your life as a student easier (if only because it will save you time) and it will also help you to become extremely employable.

Topics covered in this book

This section provides you with an overview of the topics covered in this book. This will help you to decide which chapters you need to read first. At the end of this section, you will be able to complete a self-assessment activity – a SWOT analysis – and this will provide you with a springboard to working through the rest of the book.

Chapter 2 provides guidance on personal management skills and this is an important chapter as, if you are new to higher education, it will help you to get organized and manage yourself. Topic covered in this chapter include: identifying your skills; becoming organized; managing your time; looking after yourself; managing your emotions; and gaining help and support. These skills are also valued by employers.

As suggested earlier in this chapter, studying at university requires active participation in your programme of study and for many students this involves learning new approaches to studying.

Chapter 3 provides guidance on using your higher education experiences to enhance your personal and career development. The starting point for this chapter is different approaches to learning and learning styles. If you know your learning style preferences then this enables you to capitalize on learning opportunities and also to understand your responses to particular teaching situations. Many business and management programmes provide opportunities for you to develop your professional practice by learning how to reflect and learn from different learning and practical experiences. Becoming a reflective student or practitioner will help you to capitalize on your academic experiences and also to develop yourself in the workplace. This chapter also provides guidance on developing and maintaining your portfolio as this will enable you to reflect on your progress, plan your career and have a useful source of information for job applications and interviews.

Chapter 4 provides you with guidance on studying at university. Many students find that their experience of studying at university is different to their school or college experiences, and one of the major differences is that you are expected to be responsible for your own learning and to work as an independent learner. This chapter starts with an overview of different approaches to learning and teaching and these are divided into two groups: tutor centred and student centred methods. This is followed by an overview of very common methods of learning and teaching in higher education such as:

- Lectures
- Seminars
- E-learning
- Tutorials
- Independent study.

Then there is a section on other learning and teaching methods including:

- Experiential learning
- Case studies
- Inquiry based learning (including problem based learning and work based learning)
- Action learning.

This chapter concludes with an introduction to the use of learning journals and this complements the section on reflective practice and portfolios that is presented in the preceding chapter.

At the start of your degree programme, you are likely to be familiar with using a library and finding information sources on the Internet using tools such as Google. Most students find that they need to improve and develop their information skills and, in particular, develop their skills in using academic and professional information sources. The aim of Chapter 5 is to help you to understand and use business and management information in your academic studies. This chapter provides an introduction to the ways in which knowledge is developed and disseminated in universities and research institutions. This is followed by a guide to searching and finding information using academic libraries and the Internet. Next, there is a guide to evaluating the information source and deciding whether or not to use it in your studies. After selecting appropriate items then you will need to quickly read and assess their relevance to your work. The section on academic reading skills provides guidance on obtaining the ideas and information that you require for your work. It also covers making notes. Finally, this chapter concludes with a section on referencing the work of others in your assignments.

An important topic for all students is assessment and this is covered in Chapter 6. This chapter outlines and explores a wide range of assessment activities that are used to assess students' achievement of the learning outcomes of individual courses or modules, and their degree programme. It covers assessment methods such as:

- Examinations
- Online assessment activities
- Assignments – essays or reports or case studies
- Presentations
- Oral exams or *viva voce* examinations
- Portfolio
- Assessed group work
- Projects, e.g., workplace projects
- Dissertations or theses.

This chapter also considers the important issues of plagiarism and other forms of cheating.

Chapter 7 continues the theme of assessment and it provides guidance to students who are carrying out an extended project, dissertation or independent study. This chapter covers the following topics: project management; getting the most out of supervision sessions; working within public or private sector organizations; getting started and identifying your topic; writing your research proposal; identifying your research approach; research methodologies and methods; and writing up.

Being able to work in a team is an essential skill for anyone wanting a career in business or management. Consequently, business and management programmes provide opportunities for students to develop their knowledge and skills in this area. Group work is commonly used as a means of enabling students to both experience and learn about team work. It is commonly used as an assessment method. The topics covered in Chapter 8 include:

- Reasons for using group work
- Effective student groups
- Organizing and getting the most out of meetings
- Working in diverse groups
- Virtual groups
- Common problems in group work
- Managing the emotional aspects of group work.

The ability to work in a team and, in particular, a diverse team is valued by all organizations. This means that if you develop these skills while you are at university then you are likely to become more employable.

An increasing number of business and management students take part in professional experience (through work placements or experience) or an international experience (through working or studying abroad) as a means of developing their knowledge and skills, and enhancing their curriculum vitae. These topics are covered in chapter 9 and it is divided into three sections: professional experience; study abroad; assessing the professional experience or study abroad experiences.

The final chapter is called 'Where do I go from here?' and this is concerned with three topics: gaining employment; developing your career as a reflective manager; and also keeping in touch with your subject. This chapter covers practical topics such as: writing your *curriculum vitae*; completing an application form; assessment centres; interviews; managing success and rejection. This chapter is linked to an associated website at www.openup.co.uk/businesssuccess and this will provide you with additional support in developing your career.

Making the most of this book

This book provides you with useful *knowledge* about the academic skills required to become an effective business and management student. In addition, you are provided with a series of activities and these will help you to develop your *skills* as an effective student. What is the difference between knowledge and skills? I cannot learn how to drive a car by reading a manual, although that will give me *knowledge* about driving a car. To learn to drive a car, to acquire the skill of driving,

I need to get in a car and practise driving. In a similar way, you will get the most out of this book by practising and developing your study skills. You can start off this development process using this book and the activities and self-assessment tools that are presented in it.

To get the most out of the activities and self-assessment tools you need to be honest about your strengths and this will help you to draw on them during your studies. In addition, you need to identify your weaknesses and plan how to improve in these areas. The example provided by Mike in the case study earlier in this chapter provides a good example of a real (I have changed his name to maintain his anonymity) student who identified a weakness and then used an appropriate range of support services and activities to develop his knowledge and skills of quantitative methods. Some students find it helpful to complete self-assessment tools with the help of their friends who may offer a more objective perspective. Using an honest and objective approach will help you to get the most out of the activities and self-assessment tools, starting with Activity 1.1.

Activity 1.1 What is your starting point?

The aim of this activity is to consider your starting point as a student and, as a result of reading the outline of topics covered in this book (see above), to assess your strengths, weaknesses, opportunities and challenges or threats. This is called a SWOT Strengths, Weaknesses, Opportunities and Threats analysis. You may carry out a SWOT analysis here by completing Table 1.1.

As you complete your SWOT analysis think about yourself and the knowledge and skills that you will bring with you as you start your business or management programme.

Table 1.1 SWOT analysis

Strengths	Weaknesses
(e.g., well organized, hard working, good essay writing skills)	(e.g., hate exams, tend to panic if don't understand something, hate maths!)
Opportunities	**Threats or barriers**
(e.g., everything at university, help available from study help desk, new friends, IT help desks, student union activities)	(e.g., lack of money, not sure that I'll be able to keep up, don't know way around yet, information overload)

Once you have completed the SWOT analysis, you may find it helpful to think about your strengths and how you will use them and also develop them during your degree programme. You may also look at your weaknesses and perhaps see if they are covered in this book. Skim through the contents page and identify relevant chapters. Working through these particular chapters may help you to begin to change your weaknesses into areas of strength. You will also find it helpful to look at the opportunities section of your SWOT analysis. If you find that you have not written much in this section then this may be because you are unaware of all the opportunities open to you as a university or college student. If this is the case then you may find it helpful to surf the university or college website, or to talk to friends or tutors as a way of identifying new opportunities. Finally, you need to consider the threats or challenges that you face. Most people find that these are easier to overcome if you talk to friends, tutors or special advisors, who are likely to offer you fresh ideas and support on dealing with challenges or threats.

Universities and colleges provide structured approaches to personal and professional development. These may be called personal development planning (PDP). Activities such as the SWOT analysis and the other activities included in this book may be incorporated into your personal and professional development process. If you are required to maintain a personal development folder, portfolio or e-portfolio then this type of activity may be included in it. If you develop the habit of spending some time on your personal development using the resources in this book and also those offered to you on your programme of study then you will find that it will help you to:

- Be positive about yourself and your achievements
- Identify your strengths and areas for improvement
- Integrate different aspects of your student life
- Make the best of new opportunities and resources
- Increase your effectiveness and confidence
- Develop the skills required to be a successful student
- Develop the skills required to be successful in the workplace.

In this book a whole range of activities is included and these will help you to develop your skills as a student and also be prepared for employment. The activities are:

1.1 What is your starting point?
2.1 Identifying your skills
2.2 Identifying your goals and objectives
2.3 Managing your time
2.4 Improving your time management skills
2.5 Developing your emotional intelligence

3.1 Determining your learning style
3.2 Identify your learning style preferences using the Dunn and Dunn model
3.3 Developing your skills as a reflective student
5.1 Developing your academic reading skills
5.2 Developing your note making skills
7.1 Getting started
8.1 Developing your group work skills
8.2 How well do you chair meetings?

Finally, there are additional activities on the associated website www.openup. co.uk/businesssuccess and these are associated with Chapter 10 and they will help you to identify your next steps in your career.

Summary

This chapter provides an introduction to the book and also studying a business or management degree. It provides an outline of the topics covered in this book and also those that are beyond the scope of the book. Finally, it includes a SWOT analysis to help you identify your starting points in your personal and professional development process.

2

Personal management skills

Introduction • Identifying your skills • Becoming organized • Personal goals
• Managing your time • Looking after yourself • Managing your emotions
• Gaining help and support • Summary

Introduction

The aim of this chapter is to introduce the personal management skills required to be a successful business and management student. These skills also provide the starting point for becoming an effective manager.

Studying or reading for a degree involves different approaches to learning and teaching than those commonly used in schools and some colleges. As a business and management student, you are expected to have the following characteristics:

- *Independence*, i.e., to be able to 'stand on your own feet'; work by yourself, e.g., in preparation for taught sessions and assignments; ask for help when you need it
- Willingness to *work with others*, e.g., during taught sessions and also as part of your independent study activities
- *Self-motivation* and to be in charge of your learning processes. This involves working out when, where and how you learn best. It also means being persistent and tackling subjects and topics that you find challenging
- To be *organized*, i.e., to understand the organization of your programme of

study; attend scheduled learning and teaching activities; know the dates for examinations; know when your work has to be handed in; keep up-to-date with your emails

- The ability to *work with uncertainty and change*. Universities and colleges are complex places and you will need to develop skills in dealing with information overload; information that is updated regularly; and also activities or events that take you out of your comfort zone.

These characteristics are welcomed by employers and this means that by developing the skills to become an effective student; you will also become extremely employable.

It is quite normal for new students and also for experienced students facing new challenges to feel anxious. At the start of your degree you will have the opportunity to attend induction sessions that are designed to help you settle into university life. In many universities the first year is designed to help you find your feet, adapt to university life and become an independent learner. There are different ways of managing anxiety and you will need to find an approach that works for you. Some students find it helpful to spend time organizing themselves, for example reading through essential documents and producing a diary or work plan. Some students find it helpful to share their anxieties, for example by talking with friends, family members or tutors. In contrast, some students prefer to ask for help privately – from a tutor or their personal supervisor. One of the aims of this chapter is to help you to identify the personal management skills that will help you reduce your anxiety and to become an effective business and management student. You will find that the skills you develop in managing anxiety in a university context are very useful when you start full time employment.

An additional useful information source is: Levin, P. L. (2007) *Conquer Study Stress!* Maidenhead: Open University Press.

The topics covered in this chapter include: identifying your skills; becoming organized; managing your time; looking after yourself; managing your emotions; and gaining help and support.

Identifying your skills

This section provides you with an opportunity to consider your own skills and to identify areas for development.

Activity 2.1 Identifying your skills

Complete the following personal inventory (Table 2.1) by reflecting on your skills. Rate your skills by ticking whether or not you have minimal or no skills, basic skills or advanced skills. You may like to ask a friend or tutor to discuss your results with you.

Once you have completed Table 2.1 you will have a good understanding of your strengths and also the areas for personal development. You may find it helpful to prioritize the order in which you are going to develop your skills; some students find it helpful to select one skill from each of the three groups:

- Communication skills and team working skills
- Planning skills and time management skills
- Problem solving skills and information and technology skills.

and focus on developing those skills for a month before moving on to another set of skills. In addition, you will be able to develop these skills as part of your programme of study. You may find it helpful to discuss your development process with your tutor or academic advisor. You may also be able to obtain help and advice from your university or college's specialist support centres for study skills, personal or career development.

Table 2.1 Identifying your skills
Communication skills and team working skills

Skill areas	Evaluate your performance in the following areas:	Minimal or no skills	Basic skills	Advanced skills
Communication skills	Write reports or assignments			
	Speak in public			
	Speak in meetings			
	Motivate others			
	Influence others			
	Networking			
Team working skills	Work in a diverse team			
	Share ideas and experiences			
	Listen to others			
	Support and encourage others			
	Give and receive feedback			
	Ask for help			
	Give praise			

Planning skills and time management skills

Skill areas	Evaluate your performance in the following areas:	Minimal or no skills	Basic skills	Advanced skills
Planning skills	Set goals			
	Plan and organize work			
	Make decisions			
	Liaise with others			
	Keep written records			
	Check details			
	Monitor progress			
Time management skills	Be punctual			
	Plan and organize time			
	Meet deadlines			
	Prioritize activities			
	Multitasking			

Problem solving skills and information and technology skills

Skill areas	Evaluate your performance in the following areas:	Minimal or no skills	Basic skills	Advanced skills
Problem solving skills	Identify problems			
	Analyse problems			
	Look for solutions			
	Think creatively			
	Think logically			
	Share ideas with others			
	Choose and implement a solution			
Information and technology skills	Use word processing software, e.g., Word			
	Use database software, e.g., Access			
	Use spreadsheet software, e.g., Excel			
	Use presentation software, e.g., PowerPoint			
	Use email systems, e.g., Outlook			

Skill areas	Evaluate your performance in the following areas:	Minimal or no skills	Basic skills	Advanced skills
	Use reference management systems, e.g., EndNote or RefWorks			
	Use project management systems, e.g., MS Project			
	Search the Internet using advanced search tools			
	Use social networking systems, e.g., MySpace, Facebook			
	Use Web 2.0 tools, e.g., weblogs, wiki			

Becoming organized

Successful students are organized students. They do not necessarily spend more time on their studies than other students but the time that they do spend is focused on the areas that will lead to results. Becoming organized involves managing the information that you will receive as a student, knowing what is expected of you and meeting deadlines.

You will receive lots of information as a student and before you start your programme of study or during your induction programme you are likely to receive general university information either in printed or electronic form. The aim of this information is to provide you with general guidance about university or college life and it is likely to include the following:

- General guide including maps
- Guides to accessing university library and computer systems
- Guides to university support services such as:
  - Study advice
  - Language support
  - Accommodation
  - International student support services
  - Finance
  - Counselling services
  - Careers services
  - Disability services

- Students' union information
- Sports opportunities information
- Details of volunteering or other community opportunities
- An outline of university rules and regulations, e.g., student discipline and assessment.

This is all very useful information and it is worthwhile skim reading it and then filing it away for when you need it.

Different universities and colleges organize their induction in different ways. You may be invited to attend general induction sessions that are aimed at all students. You will also be invited to attend very specific sessions that are aimed at students studying particular programmes. It is really important to attend these induction sessions as they provide a means of getting to know your university or college, your business school or department, and also vital information about your programme. They can save you a lot of time as they provide an easy way of picking up important information, and meeting your tutors and support staff. In addition, they provide opportunities to meet other students and make friends.

When you take part in the programme induction process you will receive information at two levels: general programme information, and module or course information. Different higher education institutions use slightly different words to describe their programmes of study or courses. In this book I am using the term 'programme of study' to describe a learning process that is made up of modules, courses or units and that leads to an award, for example BA Marketing, BSc Economics, BA Management and Marketing, MSc Accounting and Finance. This relationship is illustrated in Figure 2.1 where I provide an example of a three-year full time programme of study and also a four-and-a-half-year part time programme of study. As a new student, it is important to understand the structure of your programme and also which modules you are enrolled on each semester. From this information and by using the module handbooks you can identify important dates, for example when assignment are due to be handed in; when you are required to make a presentation; and the time and dates of exams. Together with your timetable of lectures, seminars, tutorials and other activities, you can put these dates into your diary or on your wall planner. This will help you to identify the structure of your weekly learning and teaching activities, and also the milestones of assessment activities – and holidays!

At the start of your studies, you will receive detailed information about your programme of study, either in printed or electronic form, and this is likely to include:

- Programme handbook
- Timetables
- Information about the courses, modules or units that make up your programme of study

Example 1: Three-year full time undergraduate degree programme

	Modules (some institutions call these courses or units)		
Year 1	Academic and professional skills	Marketing	Management and organizational behaviour
	Accounting and finance	Business environment	Human resource management
Year 2	Research methods	Decision making for managers	Business law and ethics
	Information systems	European business	Business functions
Year 3	Internet and e-commerce	International business	Strategic management
	Business project management	Dissertation	

Example 2: Four-and-half-year part time undergraduate degree programme

	Modules (some institutions call these courses or units)	
Year 1	Academic and professional skills	Marketing
	Accounting and finance	Management and organizational behaviour
Year 2	Business environment	Human resource management
	Decision making for managers	Business law and ethics
Year 3	Information systems	Business functions
	Research methods	European business
Year 4	Strategic management	International business
	Business project management	Internet and e-commerce
Year 5	Dissertation	

FIGURE 2.1 Structure of typical programmes of study

- Study guides, e.g., guides to referencing, business information sources, research methods and study skills
- Information about each module (course or units) including:
  - Aims and learning outcomes
  - Learning and teaching methods
  - Timetable
  - Week by week learning activities, e.g., in preparation for seminars or lectures
  - Indicative content
  - Assessment methods
  - Assessment criteria
  - Hand-in dates
  - Reading list
  - Details of tutors and how to contact them.

As a new student it is important to become familiar with all of this information so that you can access it when you need it.

Practical tips for getting organized

Different students will organize their academic work in different ways. The following checklist provides practical tips for getting organized:

1 Keep up to date. Check your university email address on a regular basis for any changes to teaching timetable, assessment submission dates, etc.
2 Buy and use a diary or wall planner – whichever you prefer
3 Keep a to-do list – daily, weekly, for the semester
4 Organize your study space
5 Make sure you have the right equipment and stationery
6 Set up and organise simple filing systems
7 Invest time in learning how to use a computer
8 Invest time in learning how to access and use information sources
9 Identify useful support and help services within the university/college
10 Sort out key documents and information
11 Make sure you have your module and programme handbooks
12 Identify key dates, including examination dates or submission dates for assignments; make a note in your diary of all such dates, or put them all onto your wall planner
13 Produce a work schedule – many people find it helpful to work backwards from key dates and to work out a schedule of study times.

Personal goals

Identifying personal goals and objectives is about knowing where you are now and where you want to be in one, two or three years' time. Individual students will be working towards their own individual goals over time scales that suit their personal circumstances. Spending time thinking about and then writing down your personal goals is a useful way for clarifying your overall direction in life. Once you have identified your personal goal then it is helpful to identify your objectives. Objectives are like stepping stones and help you to move forward to achieve your goal. Ideally objectives should be SMART:

- Specific
- Measurable
- Achievable
- Relevant
- Time bound.

Once you have identified your goal and objectives then you will need to consider ways in which you can work towards them. The following case study illustrates how a student identified her goal and objectives.

Case study

Jasmine's goal was to gain a first class honours degree in management. She set herself the following objectives in her second year of her course:

1   Attend every lecture and tutorial scheduled for all modules
2   Be prepared: spend at least one hour reading up in advance of each lecture or tutorial
3   Read additional materials mentioned in class within one week of the class
4   Use the library and study services at least once a week
5   Attend every optional session advertised within the department, e.g., revision sessions
6   Ask questions if she didn't understand anything mentioned in any class – ask these during the class or send the tutor an email within 24 hours
7   Ask individual tutors for feedback on how she could get higher marks for each of her assignments within a week of receiving the feedback
8   Only go out on Friday or Saturday evening
9   Go to the gym three times a week.

Each of these nine objectives was specific and measurable, i.e., you could assess whether or not Jasmine completed them; achievable, i.e., she worked out that she could achieve each one and that they fitted into both her goal and her preferred lifestyle; they were relevant to her goal, i.e., she developed them as a result of reading a guide to gaining a first; and finally they were all time bound as they took place at specific times, e.g., three times a week, or they were scheduled to happen in response to something else, e.g., attending every optional revision session. Jasmine achieved her goal of a first class honours degree and then progressed to a career in retail management.

Activity 2.2 Identifying your goals and objectives

The purpose of this activity is to enable you to identify your goals and objectives. Please complete Table 2.2.

Table 2.2 Identifying your goals and objectives

Goal
Objective 1
Objective 2
Objective 3
Objective 4

You will find it helpful to use Jasmine's case study as an example of how to identify your goal and its associated objectives. Remember to make sure that your objectives are SMART. In particular, make sure that they are timebound. You will find it helpful to write out your goal and objectives, and keep this piece of paper in a prominent place, for example in your diary or on your bedroom wall. Look at your goal and objectives every week so that you can assess whether or not you are moving towards them. Some students find it helpful to work with a friend and to give each other support as they work towards their individual goals.

Review your goal and objectives on a regular basis. You may find that you need to change your objectives over time, such as at the start of each academic year.

Managing your time

Time management is an essential skill both for students and for people in work. If you understand your strengths and weaknesses with respect to time management and if you develop effective strategies for dealing with pressures of work then this will stand you in good stead for your studies and for your future career. A useful resource on time management is: Levin, P. (2007) *Skilful Time Management*. Maidenhead: Open University Press.

All students have different pressures on their time and they need to take these into account when they are planning their work. Here are some typical examples of the different pressures some students face:

- Sue is a first year full time undergraduate student. She has a part time job (waitressing at the weekends) and likes to play football at least twice a week
- Bushra is a part time distance learning student and she has a full time job plus family commitments – two children under the age of 5 years
- Sam is a part time student who is a single parent with a full time job
- Wen is a final year student who has set up her own company selling jewelry over the Internet.
- Sumona is a part time student who lives at home and attends a dance class twice a week in a neighbouring city. She has three siblings and is very involved in their upbringing
- Sang Woo is a final year student who has a sick parent in China. She visits him every three or four weeks and is extremely worried about his health and also the stress his illness is causing the rest of the family.

Most students find that they need to make time for the following activities:

- Attending lectures, seminars and workshops
- Checking email and virtual learning environment
- Independent study
- Finding learning resources and materials
- Paid employment or voluntary work
- Sports and social activities
- Personal and family time.

It is worthwhile spending some time thinking about how you are going to manage your time as a student. The simplest approach is to use a diary or produce a weekly schedule that contains details of all your commitments for that week. You will also need to identify your study time when you are engaged in different learning activities, for example reading, group work, searching for information, working on an assignment or revision.

New students often ask how long they should be spending on their studies each week. This is a difficult question to answer as it will depend on the programme of study and also your own study skills. In the UK, a rough guide is that for every hour of taught sessions you will need to spend two to three hours on independent study. Many universities provide guidance based on the number of academic credits gained for studying a module. For example, each credit of study may correspond to a notional ten hours of student learning and you should therefore expect to spend around 200 learning hours on a 20-credit module. Information about the length of time that you are likely to be involved in independent study is often provided at induction events and it will be provided in module and/or programme handbooks. It is worthwhile finding out what the expected time commitments are for your programme of study.

Activity 2.3 Managing your time

The purpose of this activity is to help you to understand how you use your time. One approach to planning your time is to start by keeping a time log for a week. This will enable you to identify exactly how you are spending your 'spare' time. It usually surprises students when they realize how much time they *waste*! You will then be able to identify how you can organize your time. You may find it helpful to complete Table 2.3 and to identify:

- Times you will be attending taught sessions
- Times you will be able to study either independently or in a study group
- Best times for you to use a computer (at home, work or university).

Once you have completed the table then reflect on the overall pattern of your week. You may find it helpful to consider the following questions. Are you allowing sufficient time for your studies? Are you studying at your peak times in terms of intellectual energy or are you fitting your studies into times when you are tired? Are you managing to achieve a balance between your studies, part time work and social life? If you have family responsibilities, are you able to manage the balance between your studies, paid employment and family life? Do you still have time for leisure activities? Once you have developed your understanding of the best way you can manage your time then you may find it helpful to draw up a schedule to help you maintain the balance in your life. Some students find it helpful to complete this activity each semester as they find that the balance of their lives changes as they move through their degree programme.

Many students find that there are conflicts and tensions caused by the different pressures on their time, for example studying, paid employment, partying, socializing, sports activities, etc. You will have to find a sensible balance between the different pressures in your life. In addition, students often report common

Table 2.3 Managing your time

	Morning	Afternoon	Evening	Night
Monday				
Tuesday				
Wednesday				
Thursday				
Friday				
Saturday				
Sunday				

'thieves of time' and these include friends, nightclubbing, emails or online social networking. In the first few weeks of life at university it is easy to become swept into a round of parties and socializing. It is great to make new friends and to have a good social life. However, it is important to find a balance and keep up with your studies. Many students find that they have to restrict going out to parties or nightclubs to one or two nights a week in order to keep up with their academic studies. This has financial advantages too! It is very easy to turn on your computer and log onto the Internet and then spend hours responding to emails or communicating with friends and family via social networking sites. It is worthwhile limiting your time on these activities and perhaps starting them after you have completed your studies for the day. If you find that you have problems with your time management, for example, as a result of part time work or a change in your personal situation, you should raise this with your personal advisor or academic supervisor. Your personal advisor or academic supervisor may advise you to speak to a member of the university's counselling service if you require more specific support or support of a personal nature.

Once you settle into academic life, it is worthwhile reviewing your approach to time and time management. Here are some comments from current business and management students:

> I treat uni like a 9–5 job. I work in all my free sessions. The rest of the time (evenings and weekends) I do my own thing. My marks are averaging 65% so I reckon I'm doing OK.

> I meet with a friend on the same course every Thursday night. We go through our notes together and help each other with things we don't understand. We also share ideas for our assignments but work on them separately because we are frightened of being accused of plagiarism.

> I've learnt that I work best in the mornings. So, if I have an assignment then I get up early and get going with it. It means I limit nights out. I also found that if I end a study session at the end of a topic or section then it is harder to get going again. So I end mid-topic and this means I get going faster next time.

> I'm very vain and I cover my mirror in my room when I'm studying. Otherwise I spend too much time looking at myself.

> I'm a part time student and I take my core textbooks with me everywhere I go. At lunchtime, I normally get about half an hours study time. Even if I'm queuing at the doctor's surgery then I'll do my university work. Each week these bits of time add up to 5 or 6 hours of study time. It means I keep on top of my course.

These quotations indicate that studying is a personal process and different people find different strategies for making the best use of their time. Table 2.4 provides a summary of tips and strategies for time management.

Activity 2.4 Improving your time management skills

The aim of this activity is to help you develop your time management skills.

Read Table 2.4 and identify one time management tip that you are going to put into practice this coming week. At the end of the week, review your experience and on the basis of your results decide whether or not to incorporate the time

Table 2.4 Tips and techniques for time management

At regular times ask yourself 'What is the best use of my time right now?	**Emails** Check email regularly Flag up important emails Use folder facility
Searching for information Use guides to the library and electronic sources Attend workshops on using information sources Ask for help in the library (by email, phone or visiting a help desk)	**Creating the right atmosphere for studying** Organize your study space Use a 'keep out' sign on your door Switch off email, mobile phone, etc. Minimize interruptions when completing certain tasks, e.g., writing an assignment or revision Identify whether you prefer to study in a quiet or noisy atmosphere and then choose the space that best suits your needs
Technology Obtain handbooks and other information from computer centre: read them Spend time learning how to use relevant packages Attend relevant courses or workshops	**Paper work** Use Post-it notes to highlight action Use highlighter pens to mark out key information
Workloads Set realistic deadlines Say 'no' to distractions Set targets and rewards Use a daily to-do list Identify what you will achieve by the end of the day	**Prioritize** Prioritize work by organizing it under the following four headings: 1 Urgent and important 2 Important but not urgent 3 Urgent but not important 4 Not urgent and not important Alternatively items in your to-do list can be assigned a priority 1–4, based on these headings
Self-management Know your own work peaks and troughs Set your own calendar/schedule Keep your desk clear Have tea breaks and lunch breaks Speak to friends or your tutor if you feel overwhelmed	**Study groups** Set up and study with a small group of friends Talk about your studies Share feedback on assignments Give and receive support and feedback

management technique into your everyday study routines. Then choose another technique and experiment with that one in the following week. Again, review your experience at the end of the week and decide whether or not to continue using the technique in future. Working in this way and selecting a number of different tips and techniques, you will be able to develop your time management skills.

Looking after yourself

The personal situation of students varies and this is shown by the following examples:

- James is a first year business and management student who is living in hall and he has all of his meals supplied. His parents are supporting him and he has no need to earn additional money
- Anya is a Lithuanian student who has been in the UK for six months. She is living in a shared house and has to provide all her own meals. She finds shopping and cooking difficult to organize. She regularly goes to the university sports centre and is a member of the women's hockey team
- Tawfik is an Egyptian student who is living in a university owned flat. He has never cooked before he came to the UK and finds that he doesn't like the food available in the university cafes. He regularly eats out in local restaurants but finds this expensive. He goes to the gym regularly
- Christine is a single parent with two children under the age of 5 years old. She always feels that she is rushing against the clock. Although she provides good quality food for her children she rarely cooks for herself and tends to snack on the children's left over meals. Christine says that she doesn't need any exercise as she spends her whole life rushing around
- George has mental health issues and finds it difficult to shop and cook for himself. His family have disowned him and he has very limited funds. George walks everywhere as he cannot afford bus fares.

These examples indicate that every student's situation is unique and this means that you need to reflect on your own circumstances and consider how you can best look after yourself. Most students find that they quickly settle into university life and adapt to the student lifestyle. Some students find that it is difficult to look after themselves at university and this is often an issue in their first year as they are settling into a new lifestyle. All universities provide support services for students and their staff are very willing to provide help as and when required by students.

Key aspects of looking after yourself may include:

- Know your own work peaks and troughs. Most people have times of the day when they are full of energy and other times when their energy is low. For example some people are at their best in the morning while others are afternoon or evening people. If you know your energy levels are at their peak then arrange to carry out your work at these times
- Eat properly: many students skip meals or depend too heavily on fast food; eating regular meals will help you to have the right energy levels for completing your academic work and for enjoying the rest of student life
- Take regular exercise: this may involve taking part in sports activities, visiting the gym or walking to the university instead of taking a bus
- Use time management techniques (see summary in Table 2.3)
- If you feel overwhelmed speak to friends, family, staff in your home department or staff in the university's central student support services.

Managing your emotions

Working towards your degree is likely to be an emotional experience. For example you may be anxious at the start of your programme; you may receive a particularly high or low mark for an assignment; or you may have a particularly challenging time working with other students on an assessed activity. Many of the emotional experiences of student life are similar to those people experience in the workplace, consequenlty developing your ability to manage your emotions will help you in the rest of your life. One approach to exploring and managing emotions is known as developing 'emotional intelligence'.

The concept of emotional intelligence was developed and promoted by Daniel Goleman in the US during the 1990s. While there is some debate about the value of the concept of emotional intelligence, which involves traits such as social deftness, persistence and empathy, it is a practical approach to exploring and understanding emotions. In addition, it is an approach to personal development. According to Daniel Goleman (1995) emotional intelligence involves the following:

1 Self-awareness, i.e., knowing one's own emotions. The ability to identify your own emotions provides an opportunity to manage them
2 Managing emotions: the ability to identify and manage your emotions, e.g. feelings of disapointment or anger, and avoid allowing them to inappropriately impact on our lives and relationships with others
3 Self-motivation: the ability to motivate yourself and to recognize that it is

sometimes necessary to delay gratification or stifle impulsiveness in order to achieve your goals. This is particularly relevant to students who sometimes need to put aside opportunities to socialize, e.g. night clubbing, in order to study

4 Recognizing emotion in others: the ability to 'read' the emotions of others and to be empathetic

5 Handling relationships: this involves using social skills and your emotional awareness to develop and maintain constructive relationships with others.

This concept of emotional intelligence is relevant to students and it offers a useful tool for reflection. This is demonstrated in the following case study:

Case study: emotional intelligence

As part of a first year module five students were asked to work together on an assessed group project. The project involved research that had to be written up as a report and poster.

Initially, the group worked well together but as the deadline loomed, one member (Sam) became more and more stressed and began to change the structure of the report and poster that had been agreed on at the group meetings. Sam communicated these changes to the group leader, Ashish, but did not let anyone else know what he was doing. This caused tensions in the group.

Nick and Tim ignored the problems and didn't seem to care about what happened as they said they only needed to pass the first year, so getting a mark of more than 40% didn't matter to them. Jane and Wen were very upset by the situation. They wanted to get good marks and Wen had a scholarship that depended on her obtaining a 65% average score each year.

The atmosphere at each meeting got worse and worse. Jane decided to tackle the issue and raised it in the next meeting. She said she was concerned that the group was falling apart and that they would fail if they didn't all pull together. She also said that she was concerned about Wen and her scholarship.

After some discussion, the group decided to stick to decisions made in the meetings. Jane and Wen took over the editing process, while Sam was pleased that they were taking responsibility and were concerned about getting a good mark. He said that, as he'd only talked to Nick and Tim, he'd thought the whole group was aiming at 40% rather than a high mark. He agreed to focus on research. Jane's intervention helped to sort out the situation and the group ended up with a mark in the 60s.

In this case study, Jane took the lead in raising and attempting to sort out the group issues. She showed emotional intelligence in recognizing that there were problems and tackling them in an appropriate manner. She acknowledged the difficulties in a nonjudgemental way and came up with a solution that met everyone's needs.

Activity 2.5 Developing your emotional intelligence

The questionnaire presented in Table 2.5 provides a process tool that you may like to complete and use the results as a focus for reflection for personal development. Complete the questionnaire as honestly as possible. You may like to ask your friends or family for their observations too. Once you have completed the questionnaire, you may find it helpful to discuss your responses with a friend or your personal supervisor.

Individuals who have well developed emotional intelligence and who are able to manage their own emotions and are sensitive to the needs of others are often very successful in the workplace. This is because they are likely to have excellent people skills. It is worthwhile developing your emotional intelligence. One approach to developing your emotional intelligence is to identify areas in the questionnaire where you obtained a low score (i.e., never or rarely). Most people find it is possible to improve their emotional intelligence by focusing on specific areas, for example if you answered 'rarely' to question (1), you may develop this skill by noticing how you feel at regular intervals during the day. At first you many find that this is quite difficult but with practice it will become part of your natural repertoire of behaviours. Some students find emotional issues extremely difficult and, if this is your situation, then you may find it helpful to talk to a counsellor. Many universities and colleges provide specialist workshops on developing emotional intelligence and working with others.

Finally, it is important *not* to use the results of this activity to label or stereotype yourself or others. Individuals are extremely sophisticated and our emotional intelligence is not fixed. It will change during the course of our lives and as a result of our experiences at university, at work and with our families and friends.

The questionnaire in Table 2.5 is not a scientific measuring tool but a process tool that you may like to complete working by yourself, with colleagues or friends, or with a team. The results may form the focus for reflection for personal development.

When you review your answers then it is your responses to the left of the page that are worth focusing on.

Table 2.5 Emotional intelligence process tool (adapted from Allan 2006)

Aspects of emotional intelligence	Questions	Never	Rarely	Usually	Always
Self-awareness	1 I am normally aware of my feelings 2 I am aware of subtle changes in my feelings 3 I am normally aware of my body language and how it matches my feelings				
Managing emotions	4 I don't let my feelings get in the way of my relationships at work 5 If I am feeling emotional at work then I defer making important decisions 6 If I am angry then I manage my emotions so that my actions or words are not destructive				
Self-motivation	7 I am self motivated and willing to work towards my goals 8 I can delay gratification in pursuit of my goals 9 If I experience a set back then I can keep going and remain optimistic				
Recognizing emotions in others	10 I am good at 'reading' the feelings of others 11 I notice small changes in the emotions of others 12 Friends tell me that I am empathetic and understand their feelings				
Handling relationships	13 I can handle conflict and emotional upsets in groups 14 I can sense and recognize the feelings in a group 15 I can normally find the appropriate words to say to someone who is upset or angry				

Gaining help and support

Many students first ask friends or family for help and support if they meet problems in their academic life. Friends and family are a very important source of support but it is worth being aware that they may not have accurate information about student life today. This is particularly true of parents who may have graduated 25 years ago, when academic life was very different to how it is today.

Universities and colleges provide a wide range of support services for students. These services may be located within your department or faculty, or they may be central services, provided and organized by the institution. It is worthwhile getting to know the range of services that are available and also the people who provide these services.

Establishing good relationships with key people in your department will make it easier for you to ask for support and help when required. The following people are likely to be important in terms of the management of your programme of study and individual modules, courses or unit:

- Programme leader or director
- Module leader
- Tutors
- Personal supervisor
- Programme administrator
- Work placement coordinator
- Mentor.

It is likely that you will have the opportunity to meet these staff members informally at the start of the academic year and it is worthwhile taking time to get to know these key people. They are the people who will provide you with help during your programme of study and it is easier for them to help you if they get to know you. In addition, at some stage you will be asking for a reference and it is much easier for these key people to write a reference if they know you well. Here are some comments from current business and management students:

> I was seriously ill in my second year. My personal supervisor was great. She even visited me in hospital. She helped me to fill in the paperwork so that I could do my exams in the summer. Without her I wouldn't have completed my degree.

I accidentally took the wrong module – I wasn't enrolled on it but went to all the lectures and tutorials. The programme leader sorted it out for me. I thought he'd laugh and treat me like an idiot but he was very helpful. Thanks to him I didn't have to do the original module as he arranged a substitution.

I had a work placement in my third year. It was a disaster. The company was badly organised and I spent all my time in a room checking computer records. After the first week I wasn't learning anything. I e-mailed the Work Placement Co-ordinator and she sorted it out. After a few weeks, I was moved to a local authority who provided me with really good business management experience.

My programme leader was always extremely helpful and her door was always open for students. She was also very supportive through challenging times and really helped me achieve my 2:1 Honours degree.

At the university or college level there will be a number of departments or units that offer help and support to students. These include:

- Library staff
- Computer centre staff
- Study advice
- Language support
- Accommodation
- International office
- Finance
- Counselling services
- Careers services
- Disability services.

As mentioned earlier in this chapter, you will receive information about all of these services at the start of your programme of study. It is well worth making contact with and using these services as appropriate throughout your course. Here are some comments from current business and management students:

I kept having problems with the MS Project software. I must have been to the computer centre help desk at least twenty times but they helped me sort it out. They were very patient. I ended up with 85% for the project and was so thrilled I took them a box of chocolates.

I returned to study as a mature student and at first I was terrified. I hadn't studied for more than 20 years. I was very worried about my first assignment. I took it to the study advice people in the student block. They looked at my draft and showed me ways of making it 'more academic.' They also helped me with referencing. It is a confidential service which means that my tutors don't know I used it.

English is my second language. I was worried about speaking up in class. I signed up for an academic English course in the Language Support Unit. It was very helpful and gave me confidence to improve my spoken English and speak up in class in front of fellow students and the lecturers. The course also helped me with my written English for assignments.

After my first assignment, my tutor suggested that I might be dyslexic. I was shocked but went to see the Disability Service – I hate that name 'Disability' as I don't think of myself as disabled. They assessed me and I now have a mentor who gives me specialist support plus additional time in exams. Overall, it is helpful but I am still getting used to it.

Summary

The aim of this chapter is to enable you to consider the personal management skills that are required to be an effective student. These skills are also highly valuable in the workplace. Most students find that they need to spend some time developing the skills required to becoming organized, manage their time, look after themselves, manage their emotions, and gain help and support. Although university level study encourages independent learning this doesn't mean that you have to do it by yourself. There are lots of sources of help and support available to you both within your department and university.

3

Different approaches to becoming a success in the workplace

Introduction • Overview of theories of learning • Becoming a reflective learner • Making the most of different learning opportunities • Developing your portfolio • Summary

Introduction

The aim of this chapter is to provide guidance to students on different approaches to becoming a success in the workplace. Developing the knowledge and skills required in the workplace is an important part of your higher educational experiences. While you are studying for your degree you will gain up to date knowledge about your chosen areas of business or management, and you will also acquire a range of technical skills. In addition, you will learn how to become an effective learner: an essential requirement for working either in organizations or as an entrepreneur.

The rapid rate of change in organizations and at work means that the knowledge gained during your degree will soon be out of date. This means that employers are increasingly emphasizing the need for ongoing workplace learning and continuous professional development. The ability to become an effective learner as a student or a reflective practitioner (as an employee) is vitally important.

Individuals who have developed the ability to continuously learn, develop and improve their practice are extremely employable.

This chapter starts by providing an overview of theories of learning and becoming a reflective learner. Knowing about different learning styles provides you with information that you may use to help get the best out of your programme of study. As a student, you will have many opportunities to develop your knowledge and skills, for example by taking part in a range of different activities that are available at university, through employment opportunities or voluntary work, by taking up opportunities to engage in special activities such as competitions, by studying or working abroad, or by taking part in sports or other activities. It is really important to capitalize on your experiences and the final section, on developing your portfolio, will help you to make the most of these experiences.

Overview of theories of learning

Learning is a complex and messy business, and it is difficult to summarize learning theories without the risk of oversimplifying. Many business and management students are introduced to theories of learning as part of their degree programme and they discover that there is some overlap between different theories of learning. This section focuses on those theories of learning that are most relevant to students or to developing the learning skills required for the workplace.

Learning styles

The basic idea behind analysing learning styles is that each person has a preferred way of learning new topics or skills. Here are some of the different ways in which different students like to learn:

> I enjoy talking with my friends and discussing new ideas

> Reading the relevant bits of lots of different textbooks

> I start with Wikipedia as this gives a good overview. I then use the set textbooks.

I use old rolls of wallpaper and draw diagrams and show the links between different ideas.

I write down the main points in big writing and then stick them on the wall. I read them and say them out loud. I do that a few times and then write it out in my own words.

Lots of diagrams and flowcharts, and I use different colours for different topics.

I sort out my ideas while I take the dog for a walk. Once it is clear then I work out the detail.

In addition, different types of material or learning activities require different styles. For example, reading and reflecting on theories about organizational behaviour will help you to develop your knowledge and understanding of that field. In contrast, developing the skills required to manage a meeting have to be developed and mastered through experience.

There are many different models of learning styles and two of them are considered here: (1) the Honey and Mumford (1992) model is selected because it is widely used in higher education and also management education, and it is often referred to in discussions about reflection and reflective practice; and (2) the Dunn and Dunn (1999) model is included because it provides a very broad perspective on individual approaches to teaching and learning. There are extensive academic debates about the reliability and validity of different models of learning styles and, in the context of this book, I think they offer a valuable framework for thinking about individual approaches to learning.

The Honey and Mumford (1992) model was based on the ideas of Kolb (1984), and it is now widely used in academic and commercial learning and teaching situations. Peter Honey and Alan Mumford found that different people prefer different ways of learning and that most people are unaware of their preferences. They identified four main learning styles (activist, pragmatist, reflector, theorist) and suggested that individuals may work around a learning cycle (see Figure 3.1) as they tackle new subjects. The first stage in this cycle is when something happens (the action), this is then reflected upon and as a result of this reflective

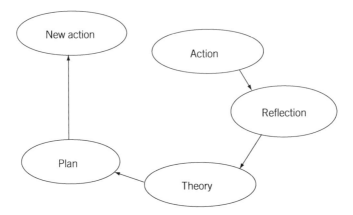

FIGURE 3.1 Learning cycle

process, the individual develops a theory. In order to put this theory into practice, a plan (the pragmatic stage) is developed and this is put into practice in a new action. Honey and Mumford produced tools for identifying individual learning styles and these are available online (http://www.peterhoney.com) and a simplified version is presented in Table 3.1. This inventory is a process development tool – it was designed to encourage reflection, and it is not a scientific measuring tool.

Activity 3.1 Determining your learning style

The purpose of this activity is to help you reflect on you preferred learning styles. Complete the questionnaire that is presented in Table 3.1. Then work out your preferred learning styles using the scoring system.

Once you have identified your preferred learning style then read the explanations that follow Table 3.1. Identify your preferred learning style and think about your learning strengths and also ways in which you could develop your approach to learning.

When you complete this self-assessment you may find that you have a strong learning preference, e.g., you score a high 6 in one area and low 1s or 2s in other areas. Alternatively, you may find that you obtain similar scores in each area. There is no right or wrong 'answer' to this learning style questionnaire. Each combination of scores brings its own mixture of strengths and weaknesses. What is important is that you reflect on your results and identify *your* strengths and weaknesses. You will then be able to capitalize on your strengths and begin to develop and convert your weaknesses into strengths.

Table 3.1 Learning styles questionnaire (based on the work of Honey and Mumford 1992)

Learning style questions	Yes	No
1 Do you find it easy to meet new people and make friends?		
2 Are you cautious and thoughtful?		
3 Do you get bored easily?		
4 Are you a practical 'hands-on' kind of person?		
5 Do you like to try things out for yourself?		
6 Do friends consider you to be a good listener?		
7 Do you have clear ideas about the best way to do things?		
8 Do you relish being the centre of attention?		
9 Are you a bit of a daydreamer?		
10 Do you keep lists of things to do?		
11 Do you like to experiment to find the best way to do things?		
12 Do you prefer to think things out logically?		
13 Do you like to concentrate on one thing at a time?		
14 Do people sometimes think of you as shy and quiet?		
15 Are you a bit of a perfectionist?		
16 Are you usually quite enthusiastic about life?		
17 Would you rather 'get on with the job' than talk about it?		
18 Do you often notice things that other people do not?		
19 Do you act first and then think about consequences later?		
20 Do you like to have everything 'in its proper place'?		
21 Do you ask lots of questions?		
22 Do you like to think things through before getting involved?		
23 Do you enjoy trying out new things?		
24 Do you like the challenge of having a problem to solve?		

A word of caution: the aim of this activity is to help you to focus your thinking on your approaches to learning. Individuals are extremely flexible and our approaches to learning change as we go through life. This means that it is important *not* to label or stereotype ourselves during this activity. Treat it as a snapshot of your preferred approach to learning at one particular time. In addition, remember that each of the four learning styles brings with them different advantages and disadvantages.

Scoring

Look at your responses to the questionnaire. Identify each question that you answered 'yes'. Note the number of the question and then circle that number in the table below. For example, if you answered 'yes' to question 14 then circle the number 14 in the reflector row. Once you have circled all the numbers relating to your 'yes' questions then add up the number of circles in each row to give your total row score.

Hint: add up the number of circles not the numbers themselves!

The row with the highest scores indicate your learning style preferences.

Table 3.2 Learning styles – scoring system

							Total
Pragmatist	4	5	11	13	17	24	
Activist	1	3	8	16	19	23	
Reflector	2	6	9	14	18	22	
Theorist	7	10	12	15	20	21	

The four different learning styles are now described and you are advised to read each of the descriptions and decide which one most closely matches your own approach to learning. It is unlikely that anyone of the descriptions will be 100 percent accurate as these descriptions are broad generalizations and so are not accurate portraits of any one person.

Pragmatists

Pragmatists take a practical approach to their studies. They want to know that what they are studying is relevant and useful to either their assessed work and/or the workplace. They enjoy practical tasks and activities such as case studies and problem based learning. They don't enjoy abstract theories particularly if they can't see their relevance to everyday life. Pragmatists prefer action rather than longwinded discussions and they want to 'get on with the job'. They often ask questions about the relationships between what they are studying and 'real life'.

Activists

Activists will often dive into situations and 'get on with it'. They enjoy learning through activities, case studies or work based learning, and they can quickly become bored if there is too much discussion or theory. Activists tend to enjoy practical activities and opportunities to do something creative or different. They are less keen on detailed research and planning activities, when they may become bored rather quickly. Many activists don't like to work by themselves as they prefer to be part of a group and enjoy the social side of learning.

Reflectors

Reflectors like time and space to think things through carefully before coming to a conclusion. They are most comfortable when they have access to all the relevant information and time to make a considered decision. Reflectors are very good at working through a problem or set of ideas, and they will often identify issues that other people have not noticed. They sometimes find it hard to keep to deadlines as they need to consider all the relevant information and every possibility. In addition, they may become frustrated if asked to complete activities over a very short time span as this doesn't provide them with sufficient time to think or reflect on the subject. Some reflectors appear to be quiet or shy, however this is because they are thinking deeply about the topic. Reflectors are often extremely uncomfortable if they are put on the spot and asked to voice their opinion. They need time to think and reflect on the topic.

Theorists

Theorists like to know the reasons behind things, and they have a methodical and logical approach to their subject. They like to analyse ideas in a logical way and they will ask questions and make mental connections until they have integrated new ideas or theories into their existing knowledge. They are not usually happy with subjective judgements or making decisions on the basis of scant evidence. Theorists are often perfectionists with set ways of doing things and this can mean that they find it frustrating if they are dealing with contradictory information. They pay attention to detail and this is a great strength but it can also slow them down and prevent them completing their work on time.

Learning styles theories are commonly introduced to business and management students and you may be asked to explore and critique them as part of one of your modules or units of study. In the context of this book, it is worth noting some of the limitations to this model which was developed in the context of Western approaches to management training in organizations. The model offers an oversimplification of the learning process, for example Figure 3.1 suggests that learners move around a cyclical process in a linear manner. My own experience is that learning is a more complex process than is implied by the model; students may move around the cycle in a variety of directions and spend varying amounts of time at different stages. In addition, individual learners may be involved in a number of processes at the same time, for example my own style of reflection is through activities such as writing or talking. Despite these limitations, the model does have the benefit of providing a simple framework that students may use to explore and reflect on their own experiences.

The Dunn and Dunn (1999) model of learning styles (see Table 3.3) was developed by researchers in the US who identified seven aspects of learning: perceptual, information processing, problem solving, environmental, physiological, emotional and sociological. The characteristics of each of these elements are outlined in Table 3.3.

Activity 3.2 Identify your learning style preferences using the Dunn and Dunn model

The purpose of this activity is to help you reflect on you preferred learning styles. Complete the questionnaire that is presented in Table 3.3, which is divided into four sections:

1　Perceptual and Information processing
2　Problem solving and environmental
3　Physiological and emotional
4　Sociological.

You may decide to complete the whole questionnaire at once or work through one section at a time. Completing the questionnaire will help you to identify the different ways in which you prefer to study. Once you have identified your preferred learning styles then you may find it helpful to play to their strengths, for example when revising for examinations. It is also worthwhile exploring and developing the approaches to learning that are not your strengths, as this will help you to become a more flexible learner. It may also help you to do well on *all* your modules or units of study rather than just on those that match your learning style preferences. One approach to developing your learning strengths is to practice learning and studying using a range of different methods. Some students find it helpful to work with other students who have different learning style preferences to their own ones as this helps them to learn from each other.

These two models of learning styles are relevant to students as they provide insights into individual learning style preferences. You may find it helpful to identify your learning style preferences and this knowledge will help you to capitalize on your strengths and also to develop your ability to learn in areas that are not your preferred style. Most students find that they particularly enjoy some lecturer's modules and courses and this may be because the lecturer's learning style preferences matches those of the student; this makes for a very positive learning experience. However, if there is a mismatch, for example the lecturer includes many group based activities but the student has a preference for individual learning activities, then the student may need to work harder in order to gain full benefit from the teaching methods. While some students may find this a negative experience, in reality it provides an important opportunity for personal development.

Table 3.3 Dunn and Dunn Learning Style Model

	Learning style preference	Statements	Please tick below to indicate the statements that most describe your approaches to learning
Perceptual and information processing			
PERCEPTUAL – individual preferences for taking in information	Auditory	I enjoy learning by listening to others and through discussions	
	Visual – image	I enjoy learning using diagrams, flowcharts, pictures	
	Visual – text	I prefer to learn by reading a book, article or information on the web	
	Tactile or kinaesthetic	I prefer to learn by being active or moving, e.g., hands-on, creating physical models	
INFORMATION PROCESSING – individual preferences for processing or organizing information	Analytic	I prefer to learn by working through a new topic in a step by step manner	
	Global	I prefer to learn by understanding the 'big picture' or overview before I go into details	
	Combined – analytic and global	I prefer to learn using a combination of methods of understanding the big picture and working through the details step by step	
Problem solving and environment			
PROBLEM SOLVING – individual preferences for solving problems, e.g., tackling assignments	Reflective	I prefer to tackle problems or assignments by thinking about what is required	
	Impulsive	I like to tackle problems by enthusiastically leaping in and working on them	

(Continued Overleaf)

Table 3.3 Continued

	Learning style preference	Statements	Please tick below to indicate the statements that most describe your approaches to learning
ENVIRONMENTAL – what kind of environment do you like to study in?	Sound	I like to study with background music	
		I like to study in a quiet environment	
	Light	It is important to me to study in an environment where I can adjust the light to suit my preferences	
	Temperature	It is important to me to study in an environment where I can adjust the temperature to suit my preferences	
	Seating	I like to study sitting in a chair	
		I like to lounge about on a sofa or bed when I am studying	
Physiological and emotional			
PHYSIOLOGICAL	Time of day	I study best in the morning	
		I study best in the afternoon	
		I study best in the evening	
		I study best during the night	
	Intake	I like to nibble at food when I am studying	
		I prefer not to eat when I am studying	
	Mobility	I like to move around when I am studying	
		I am comfortable sitting still when I am studying	
EMOTIONAL	Motivation	I am self-motivated in my studies	
		I need to be motivated by others, e.g., friends and tutors, to help me study	
	Persistence	I can persevere with my studies even when I am finding them difficult	
		I easily give up if I come across problems	

	Conformity	I am comfortable following the instructions of my tutor
		I prefer to do things my own way
	Structure	I like well organized and clearly structured learning activities
		I prefer to decide how I am going to carry out a learning activity. I find instructions constrain me
Sociological		
SOCIOLOGICAL	Team	I prefer to work by myself
		I enjoy working in small groups of two or three students
		I enjoy working in large groups of four to eight students
	Authority	I prefer to ask my tutor for advice or help
		I prefer to ask friends for advice or help
		I make up my own mind as to how to deal with problems
	Variety	I like modules or courses to be run in a consistent manner so I know what to expect
		I like variety and change in my modules and courses.
		I don't like it when the teaching sessions become predictable

Becoming a reflective learner

> Reflection is an important human activity in which people recapture your experience, think about it and mull over it and evaluate it. It is this working with experience that is important in learning. The capacity to reflect is developed it different stages in different people and it may be this ability which characterizes those who learn effectively from experience.
>
> (Boud et al., 1987:19)

As a business or management student, you will be expected to take charge of your own learning experiences and also your career development. You will need to develop the skill of evaluating your own progress, your strengths and weaknesses, and also to decide which areas of development to focus on. One important source of feedback is that provided by your lecturers and tutors, for example through marks or grades, written feedback on assignments or presentations, and verbal feedback in seminars. In addition, it is important for you to develop the ability to work out for yourself, through a process of analysis and reflection, what you do well and what you need to do to improve.

The ability to reflect on and learn from your experiences is important to enable you to learn from all your activities (academic, employment, work placements, social life) and it forms the basis for personal learning and change. Reflection is the act of thinking about a particular experience or event. It may involve:

- Reflection in action, i.e., thinking about the experiences as it is taking place
- Reflection on action, i.e., thinking about the experience after it has happened.

The aim of reflection is not to justify what has happened but to attempt to understand it and learn from it. Reflection is concerned with probing or exploring something that has happened so that you gain new insights or a better understanding of the situation and also so that you learn from it and change the way in which you act in future. Reflection is often emphasized in management programmes as it forms the basis of much management learning in the workplace. The starting point for reflection is often to look at a problem, something that causes discomfort or conflict, or evokes an emotional response. This may then lead to the type of learning cycle described in Figure 3.1, where reflection on a specific action leads to the development of a personal theory, which will then be translated into some kind of practical approach or plan for dealing with the situation and so results in a change in our behaviour (or action). This is illustrated in the following case study.

Case study: reflection in practice	
A second year student James was asked by his tutor to present a seminar with a student called Laura. The topic was 'buyer behaviour in supermarkets in the UK and China'. They gained a distinction for their work.	
Action	James hadn't worked with Laura before and found that she was very 'fussy' and wanted every detail of the seminar worked out beforehand. Consequently, they spent a long time in preparing for the seminar.
Reflection on action	James reflected on his work (or action) and noted that he had spent longer than normal on preparing for the seminar. In addition, he had read many more articles than his norm. Laura's approach had forced him to tackle the work in a much more detailed way than his normal style.
Theory	James developed a working theory that planning and research led to improved grades.
Plan	James decided that in future he would spend more time on his assignments and also use a larger range of references. He would also see if he could work with Laura on future projects.
New action	James put his plan into action and he gained a much higher mark than normal for his assignment. This confirmed his working theory.

How to manage the reflective process

Most people reflect on their daily experiences – as they travel home, in the shower or at the gym. Many students find it helpful to reflect on a regular basis and some important methods of reflection include:

- Keeping a learning journal or diary
- Maintaining a personal portfolio, e.g., an e-portfolio
- Reflecting on feedback on assessed work
- Completing personal development activities such as the learning styles inventories presented earlier in this chapter.

Learning journals or logs are particularly useful for capturing many of the incidents or incidental events that are soon forgotten as the academic year progresses. These logs may be kept as a private and individual learning tool, and there is no right or wrong way to keep them. Find the method that suits you, and remember the following points:

- Write what is important to you: it is important to be yourself
- Be open and sincere in what you record
- The log is a working document: as it develops, go back to earlier entries and reflect further on them, underlining, highlighting, annotating anything significant
- Remember to date all entries
- Don't be rigid in the way you keep your log: be prepared to change if necessary, moulding the log to fit your personal strengths and needs
- Record experiences as soon as possible after they happen, but be selective: focus on experiences that are significant for you or critical to the project.

One way of ensuring that reflection takes place is to decide on a regular time at which you will write your log, and a fixed time each week to reflect back on it. It is not just writing in the log that is important, but the continuing reflection on what you have written. The following questions (which are not exhaustive) may suggest things you might write about as you keep your learning diary. Choose one set of questions and use them as a tool for reflection. They are only intended as a stimulus to help you focus on *your* experience and *your* reflection on it.

1 Are things going to plan? If not, why not? What do I need to do differently?
2 How do I feel about this module? What am I enjoying? What do I dislike? What do I need to do differently?
3 How do I feel about this assignment? What am I enjoying? What do I dislike? What do I need to do differently?
4 How do I feel about this assessed group work? What am I enjoying? What do I dislike? What do I need to do differently?
5 What are the gaps in my knowledge or skills in relationship to this module? How can I develop my knowledge and skills? Who will help me?
6 Select a critical incident. Briefly describe it. What contributed to this situation? What was my role in creating this situation? What do I need to do differently in future?

A quick method of maintaining a learning diary of log is to keep a notebook and on a daily or weekly basis write in one piece of paper which is divided into four sections as shown in Figure 3.2.

Another approach to keeping a learning diary is through a weblog where each entry in the blog acts as an individual piece of reflection.

Programme or module activity: Date:

What went well?	What could be improved?
What have you learnt?	What will you DO as a result of this reflective activity?

FIGURE 3.2 Example structure for a learning diary entry

Activity 3.3 Developing your skills as a reflective student

The purpose of this activity is to enable you to start reflecting on your study skills. Think about one specific learning activity on your course, e.g. a lecture, seminar or workshop, and then complete the following questions (think about the experience from your perspective as a student):

What went well? (*e.g., Were you on time and fully prepared for the event? Were you able to take good notes? Did you ask questions? Did you engage in the activities?*)	**What could be improved?** (*e.g., Did you lose concentration part way through the session? Did you switch off from the session? Did you pretend to understand something rather than ask a question?*)
What have you learnt? (*What have you learnt from thinking about what went well and what could be improved? What did you learn about study skills from reflecting on the learning session?*)	**What will you DO as a result of this reflective activity?** (*This is a really important question. What will you change about the way in which you take part in this kind of study session in future? Identify what you will do differently as a SMART objective.*)

Making the most of different learning opportunities

Making the most of opportunities in higher education

Each year there are thousands of new business and management graduates all seeking employment. It is becoming increasingly important for individual students to make themselves stand out from the crowd, and one way of achieving this is to take advantage of all the different learning opportunities offered in the university or college. Here are some of the different opportunities to extend your experience that are commonly available within business schools and universities:

- Learning a new language
- Developing your information and communication skills
- Working as a student ambassador
- Working as a student mentor
- Taking part in student competitions, e.g., within a department, university or interuniversity challenges
- Working as a student representative
- Taking part in the management of a student society
- Studying abroad
- Taking part in a focus group.
- Taking part in accreditation events or other quality assurance processes
- Producing student newsletters or newspapers
- Organizing special events, e.g., Chinese New Year celebration, talent competitions
- Working as a volunteer in a local charity

Leading or taking part in a range of different events and activities will help you to develop your knowledge and skills, as well as providing practical experiences that are very relevant to the workplace.

Here is an example from a management student's portfolio:

> During my second year on my BA Management programme I passed all my taught modules with an average grade of 66%. This means that I am on target to achieve a 2:1 degree. At the same time, I organised the Chinese New Year celebrations and I was responsible for marketing this event (budget = £1000) and organising the entertainment. 500 students attended the event and we made a profit of £1200. The experience enabled me to demonstrate my leadership and organisational

skills. I was also a member of the Business School's team that entered the Young Entrepreneur 2008 competition. We reached the semi-finals and were Highly Recommended. This competition provided me with experience in working in a challenging competitive environment and making business decisions based on limited amounts of data. My third opportunity was in the area of publishing and communications as I was the editor for the student magazine, *The Biz*, which comes out each semester. As well as commissioning articles, I was also responsible for ensuring that the content was well written, accurate and suitable for the publication. This required me to pay attention to detail and also to be extremely diplomatic with some enthusiastic student reporters.

Employment

Many students work and earn money either during their time at university or during vacation time. Many business and management programmes offer opportunities for a work placement or professional experience placement (see Chapter 9). These employment opportunities enable you to:

- Gain practical work experience
- Gain experience of working within an organization
- Develop your knowledge and skills of a particular sector
- Gain experience of working in a team or independently
- Earn money!

It is worthwhile keeping a record of your work experiences as they can be used in job applications (see creating and maintaining your portfolio later in this chapter). In addition, they may be used in your academic studies as illustrated in the following example:

Julie worked as a shelf stacker in a local supermarket. In the course of eighteen months, the supermarket chain changed owners three times. Each of these changes involved the shop workers changing their employer and conditions of service, and they also had to work to new policies and practices. For her thesis, Julie researched the motivation of shop workers and she used her work experiences and those of her colleagues in the store as the focus of her study. She had to obtain ethics clearance from both the university and the store manager. Julie gained a high grade for her thesis and she later obtained employment as a trainee human resources officer in one of the major supermarket chains.

Voluntary work

Another way of gaining valuable experience and skills is through carrying out voluntary work. Volunteering opportunities are available around the world and volunteers may work a few hours per week or a few months in the summer. Many voluntary organizations require help and expertise (e.g., administration, project management, marketing, training, customer services), and many will pay travel expenses and some provide access to high quality training courses for their volunteers. Volunteering provides opportunities to:

- Gain practical work experience
- Gain experience of working within an organization
- Develop your knowledge and skills of a particular sector
- Gain experience of working in a team or independently
- Gain experience of working in a particular sector
- Give something back to a community.

Here are two examples of business and management students volunteering:

I'm studying a logistics degree but there are no jobs where I live. I volunteer for a humanitarian aid charity and work there 2 hours a week. My job is sorting out medicines and other health care products, packing them, and labelling them so that they can be sent to Afghanistan. I've learnt a lot in the job: attention to detail; the medicine's databases; and some of the export requirements for medicines. The charity send out between seven and ten million pounds of aid each year and I think this experience will look good on my CV.

I work in a charity for people with disabilities each holiday when I help with the office administration. I help with the monthly financial reports and also take minutes for meetings and write reports. I also help people use the computers and search the Internet. I sometimes fill in forms for the clients.

Sports and other societies

Another benefit of university life is having opportunities to take part in a wide range of sporting and other activities. Many students help to organize sporting events and/or are on the committee of a particular society. Engaging in these types of activities helps to demonstrate organizational skills as well as the ability to work in a team:

José played rugby and was a member of the university rugby club. He ended up on the committee as treasurer for two years. He enjoyed his sport and also the social life that went with it. When José began looking for work in an accountancy company he found that his rugby experiences provided a good topic of conversation during interviews. He obtained a trainee post with a company where there was a strong sports club.

Developing your portfolio

A portfolio is a physical or electronic file where you keep information about yourself. In many universities and colleges the concept of a student's portfolio is linked to the idea of personal development planning (PDP), which is explored in Chapter 1. Many students have the opportunity to develop their portfolio in a managed way throughout their degree programme and sometimes these portfolios are assessed and count towards their final degree award. Even if you don't have to keep a portfolio as part of your programme of study, you will probably find it helpful to keep one. They can be used in the following ways:

- To keep a record of your personal achievements and experiences
- To help you apply for jobs or interviews as your portfolio will contain up to date information about you
- As a tool that will help you to organize your personal development and reflect on it.

How to create and maintain your portfolio

As a business and management student, it is important to find out whether or not you are required to keep a portfolio as part of your course. If you are required to create and maintain a portfolio then you will need to find out what you are expected to put in it and how to present your personal development process. In the absence of specific guidelines, creating and maintaining a portfolio normally involves the following:

- Deciding whether to keep a physical portfolio or an electronic portfolio. Many virtual learning systems provide a personal space for students to keep their

portfolio. If you create and maintain an e-portfolio then make sure that you have a backup copy
- Deciding what to put in your portfolio. Many students keep the following items in their portfolio:
  - Personal development activities, e.g., completion of a personal SWOT analysis (see Chapter 1) – these may be carried out as part of a structured PDP process
  - Self-evaluation questionnaires, e.g., a skills inventory (see Chapter 2); learning styles inventories (see Chapter 3)
  - A detailed *curriculum vitae* (see Chapter 10)
  - A detailed record of their academic achievements
  - Copies of certificates and transcripts
  - A personal statement of 250–500 words which provides a summary of who you are, your career interests and achievements, and your longer term goals
  - Details of all work experiences and work placements including dates worked, salary, brief job description, your roles and responsibilities, any special activities or project work, a brief reflection on what you learned from the experience
  - Reflection on the results of self-evaluation questionnaires, personal development activities and other experiences, e.g., work experience, results from academic assessment activities
  - Photographs and other useful evidence, e.g., relevant leaflets or pamphlets
- Update your portfolio at least twice a year and whenever you have something new to add to it.

Summary

This chapter provides guidance on using your higher education experiences to enhance your personal and career development. Knowledge of the different ways in which you prefer to learn are helpful as this enables you to capitalize on learning opportunities and also to understand your responses to particular teaching situations. The development of skills as a reflective student or practitioner are vital for making the most of your academic experiences and also developing yourself in the workplace. Many modules or courses provide opportunities to learn the skills of reflection.

Developing a successful career in business or management requires more than academic knowledge and skills, it also involves making the most of a wide range of opportunities that you come across as a student, in the workplace and in other aspects of your life. Portfolios provide an important means of bringing together different aspects of your life and keeping a record of them either in a physical or electronic folder. Developing and maintaining your portfolio (PDP) will enable you to reflect on your progress, plan your career and have a useful source of information for job applications and interviews.

4

Studying at university

Introduction • Tutor centred and student centred approaches to teaching and learning • Making the most of lectures • Contributing to seminars • Using e-learning • Getting the most out of tutorials • Independent study • Experiential learning • Working on case studies • Inquiry based learning • Action learning • Learning and developing using a learning journal • Summary

Introduction

The aim of this chapter is to provide you with guidance on studying at university. Many students find that studying at university is different to school or college study, and one of the major differences is that you are expected to be responsible for your own learning and to work as an independent learner.

This chapter starts with a simplified overview of different approaches to learning and teaching: tutor centred and student centred methods. This is followed by an overview of common methods of learning and teaching in higher education. This section starts by outlining some of the commonest methods of teaching and learning in business and management education, in other words lectures, seminars, e-learning, tutorials and independent study. This is followed by an introduction to other methods including experiential learning, case studies, inquiry based learning (including problem based learning and work based learning) as well as action learning. This section is completed with an introduction to the use of learning journals and this complements the section on reflective practice and portfolios that is presented in Chapter 3.

Tutor centred and student centred approaches to teaching and learning

Business and management students come from a variety of educational backgrounds and from many different countries and cultures. This means that at the early stages of their programme of study, some students will experience different and unfamiliar approaches to learning and teaching. The aim of this section is to enable you to understand the approaches to teaching and learning that you may experience during your business or management degree programme.

There are two main approaches to teaching and learning. The tutor centred approach, sometimes called the transmission or banking model, is based on the idea that learning involves 'filling up' the learner with knowledge. In this approach to teaching the lecturer is considered to be an expert who transfers their knowledge via lectures to the student whose job is to learn everything that is presented to them. This means that the student's role is rather passive – they are a little like a container waiting to be filled. Typical examples of tutor centred learning and teaching activities include didactic lectures and also traditional computer aided learning packages based on the idea of 'drill and practice'. Examples of learning programmes that are underpinned with this approach to learning include some web based training programmes that transmit chunks of knowledge to the learner, and then use question and answer techniques or activities to reinforce the learning. One common feature of this approach to learning is that the learner has little choice about what they will learn. Tutor centred approaches are sometimes linked to an underlying theory of teaching and learning called behaviourism in which learning activities and processes are clearly labelled, observed and measured. These are typified by:

- Very specific definition of learning objectives
- Material broken down into small chunks and linked in a clear logical sequence
- Emphasis on knowledge and skill reproduction
- Learning activities sequenced by the tutor
- Frequent tests or reviews that test the ability to reproduce key facts or ideas
- Little awareness or allowance for individuals' perspectives or experiences.

This approach to teaching and learning is relevant in certain types of situation where students are required to learn specific information (e.g. definitions of terms, mathematical equations). However, they are less relevant to situations, common in business and management, where the students needs to deal with complex situations or conflicting data sets or information.

Student centred approaches to teaching and learning focus on enabling individuals to experience active and relevant learning experiences. There are three characteristics of student centred learning:

- The student is actively involved in the learning process
- Learning is based on real life and authentic situations
- Learning is treated as a social process.

This approach is linked to the concept of deep and surface approaches to learning (for example see Entwistle 1981). Individuals who adopt a deep approach to learning are concerned with the meaning of what they are studying and the ways in which an idea will fit into existing knowledge structures. Consequently, they develop a much deeper and more complex understanding of their subject. In contrast, individuals who adopt a surface approach to learning are concerned with remembering the topic (e.g., for an examination) and so have a limited grasp of the subject. The implication for students is that by becoming actively involved in the subject and working towards understanding the meaning of the ideas that they are studying they are more likely to develop a deep understanding of the subject. A wide range of group learning processes is used to encourage deep learning and examples covered in Chapter 4 include working on case studies, 'live' projects and action learning, and in Chapter 8, working in groups.

In student centred learning the learning programmes are likely to begin by identifying the learner's starting position (e.g., their current knowledge and skills) and then by identifying their goals and outcomes. The learning process is likely to be based on real life and authentic situations that are relevant to the individual learners. This process may involve the learners in discussions about their starting points and learning requirements, and it may mean that they identify how they will achieve their learning goals. Consequently, learning becomes a negotiated process that involves dialogue between learners and tutors. In the student centred model of learning, individuals learn as a result of interactions with others and what we learn depends on who we are, what we want to become and what we value. This means that learning is placed within the context of a group or a community, and it will involve activities such as group work, case studies or problem based learning.

Many students studying business and management find that their programme of study involves a mixture of both tutor centred and student centred learning activities. Table 4.1 provides a classification of different teaching methods according to whether they are tutor centred or student centred. Some methods (e.g., seminars) may be placed in each category depending on the way in which they are facilitated. Different lecturers or tutors will have their own approaches to teaching their modules and courses. In addition, the different disciplines of business and management (e.g., accounting, finance, law, management, marketing) tend to use their preferred approaches to teaching and learning. This means that

Table 4.1 A simplified summary of different methods of learning and teaching in business and management education

Tutor centred methods	Student centred methods
Lectures	Experiential learning
Many seminars	Action learning
Many tutorials	Inquiry based learning (including problem based learning
Some approaches to e-learning	and work based learning)
	Case studies
	Learning journals
	Some seminars
	Some tutorials
	Some approaches to e-learning

business and management students need to be flexible and adapt to the range of learning and teaching methods that they experience on their programmes. Working through a learning styles inventory (such as the Dunn and Dunn model presented in Chapter 3) will help you to identify your preferred teaching methods and also those that you may find more challenging.

Making the most of lectures

In lectures you are likely to be in a large group of students listening to a member of staff (tutor or lecturer) giving a talk on a specific topic. Lectures are often used to provide an overview of a subject and to identify key themes and issues. The lecturer will normally use a PowerPoint presentation and may provide a handout to identify the key points. There may be limited opportunities to ask questions. During a lecture it is a good idea to make notes of key points and ideas.

The best way to make the most of lectures is to be prepared. Lecture PowerPoint presentations and handouts are frequently available in advance (e.g., via the virtual learning environment), and it is worth obtaining these and reading through them. This helps you to become familiar with the main ideas and also the terminology. If there are any words that you don't understand then look them up in a dictionary. If there is some prelecture or preparatory reading then make sure that you do this in advance of the lecture.

It is important to arrive at the lecture on time and many lecturers will not allow late arrivals into the lecture theatre. Make sure that you have the right equipment with you (e.g. paper and pen, or laptop computer) and switch off your mobile phone. Make notes during the lecture. Don't attempt to copy down everything that the lecturer says during the lecture as you will find it an impossible task. Instead, identify key points and ideas, and also note any additional references.

Increasingly, lecturers include activities as part of their lecture sessions. The purpose of these activities is normally to help the students to actively engage in the content of the lecture. Example activities may include a quiz, an exercise, a minicase study or a discussion topic.

Audience response systems are commonly seen on TV games programmes where members of the audience use a handheld set to answer multiple choice questions or to vote on an issue. The use of these systems is becoming increasingly popular in educational settings where lecture rooms are fitted out with the appropriate technology. You may find that you are asked to use an audience response system as a way of interacting with the lecturer during the lecture. Evaluation of the use of this type of system normally shows that students enjoy using them and find that they help to make the lecture more interesting.

There is often an opportunity to ask questions either in the whole group during the lecture or individually at the end of the lecture. If the lecturer has to rush off to teach another class then email them your queries. Most lecturers really enjoy students' questions as they demonstrate that you are interested in their specialist subject, so don't hesitate to ask questions.

Making notes in lectures

Different people make notes in different ways and everyone develops their own style. What is important is that you find and use a method that works for you. Many lecturers provide access to their PowerPoint presentations in advance of the lecture. It is worthwhile printing them off and skimming through them before the lecture. Listen to what the lecturer is saying and highlight the main points plus any additional points. You should end the lecture with a clear summary that includes the key points and details about the original sources of information used by the lecturer. These information sources will then provide a useful starting point for reading more widely around the topic.

Advice on how to make notes

- Start with background details, e.g., lecture notes should include the module title, the date, the title of the lecture, and the lecturer
- It is usually impracticable to try and copy all the information presented to you during a lecture: make a summary of key ideas and themes
- Make sure you can read your notes
- Only use one side of the paper: this makes it easier to organise your notes for planning or revision

- Leave spaces for additional notes or comments
- Use arrows, symbols, diagrams: this will speed up the note-making process.

Spend some time after the lecture reviewing your notes and, if necessary, rewrite any sections that are not clear. Ask yourself some questions, such as:

- Is there anything I can add?
- Is there something that I might benefit from discussing with a fellow student or tutor?
- Should I do some additional reading on the topic?

Finally, you may find that in the early days of your study programme you make lots of notes, but as you become more experienced you might make fewer and more specific notes.

Contributing to seminars

Seminars involve smaller groups of students (i.e., 5 to 15 students) coming together with a tutor. Seminars normally focus on a particular topic and issue, and these are normally advertised in advance (e.g., in the course or module handbook). Individual students may be asked to prepare for the seminar by reading a particular article or book, working on a case study or by making a short presentation to the group.

Seminars are very important as they give you the opportunity to discuss and debate ideas with your tutor and peers. Talking about the subject will help you to sort out ideas and the evidence that supports them. This also makes it easier to write up assignments or prepare for future exams as you will have gained experience of putting ideas into your own words.

You will find it easier to contribute to seminars if you prepare for them by reading the relevant information sources (e.g., chapter in a book, case study, or journal article). Join in the discussions as early as possible during the seminar. The more you know the topic and have prepared for the seminar then the easier you will find it to speak during the seminar.

If you are asked to make a presentation, it is vital to prepare it beforehand (see Chapter 6). If you are going to use visual aids such as a PowerPoint presentation then make sure you know how to use the equipment in the seminar room. It is perfectly acceptable to take notes with you to help you during your seminar. If you are leading the seminar then when you have got to the end of your presentation it is traditional to ask, 'Any questions?' This question is often received by silence and there are a few strategies that help to manage question time.

First, you may ask a couple of friends to ask pre-prepared questions that you have given them to help start off the discussion. Another strategy is to ask your fellow students to discuss your presentation with their neighbours, in small groups, and that they need to ask a question or make a comment about your seminar presentation. Then give them a few minutes to discuss your presentation. Go around the groups and ask for their questions or comments. This approach often helps to generate questions. Finally, another option would be to hand out cards at the start of your presentation and then ask your fellow students to write down their questions or comments as they listen to your presentation. At the end of the presentation, give everyone a few minutes to write down their questions or comments; collect them in; and then respond to them.

Using e-learning

Most universities and colleges now provide students with access to a specialist Internet based e-learning environment that provides a virtual space where students may find information, receive online assessment and communicate with each other. Access to these systems, such as Blackboard, WedCT, Moodle or Sakai, is via the Internet and requires a user ID and password. New students will probably need to spend some time learning how to use their department or business school's system, and help will be provided by support services such as the library or computer centre.

The organization of the virtual learning environment will vary from university to university, but typically they are organized around individual courses or modules. Many tutors use these systems as a means of communicating with students, disseminating student handbooks and course materials, and providing access to online communication tools. Some tutors use the online assessment facilities for tests. It is important to spend some time at the start of your studies getting to know the virtual learning environment, as you will need to access it on a daily basis to obtain up to date information about your programme of study. The type of information that is available for each course or module is likely to include some or all of the following facilities:

- Announcements, e.g., about timetable or room changes, clarification of issues raised by students
- Learning materials and information sources, e.g., course or module handbooks, lecture notes, seminar papers and web links

- Discussion groups: these provide a discussion facility under various topic headings. They allow you to take part in a virtual classroom experience. This means that you will use it for tutor- or student-led discussions and activities. Messages sent to a discussion group are visible to everyone who has access. If you want to send private messages to your tutor or individual students then use email
- Conference or chat rooms provide a 'real time' text based conferencing facility (much like Internet chat or a face to face seminar). In the context of a particular course or module your tutor may use this facility to hold real time meetings or to set up syndicate work for groups of students
- Weblogs provide a means of personal expression and sharing information and thoughts. In some respects a weblog is rather like an online diary or journal which an individual uses to share their experiences. The structure of weblogs varies, but typically they are divided into two or three columns. One column (the central one) normally includes postings or brief paragraphs of opinion, information or personal diary entries and these are arranged chronologically with the most recent first. In addition, they may contain a contents list, a space for visitors to add a comment below a specific blog entry, and other features, e.g., search tool, favourite web links, etc.
- A wiki is a webpage that can be edited by any reader. One of the commonest examples of wiki is Wikipedia. One of the strengths of wiki is that they provide an opportunity for a large number of people to contribute to a set of ideas and develop a resource. The obvious disadvantage is that there is no editorial control over the material so the quality of the information is variable. Wiki are sometimes used as a tool to support group work, e.g. a group of students working together may use a wiki and produce a wiki based online report.

Learning to work effectively as a student in a virtual learning environment takes time. For students new to this approach to learning it is worthwhile spending some time exploring the site and becoming familiar with its layout and the online tools. Many business and management programmes involve group work and this may take place in an online environment. This is a useful learning experience as many multinational organizations function using a range of virtual teams and so developing skills in virtual team work is likely to enhance your employability skills. An important skill in online group or team work is the ability to take part in online discussions. As with face to face meetings there are some standard approaches to working together in an online environment. Many of the ideas in this section come from the work of Salmon (2000).

Getting started

You will need to start with introductions and get to know each other. Remember the rules of netiquette (online etiquette).

- Be polite
- Keep it brief
- Acknowledge each other
- Respond to each other's messages
- Don't be too concerned about spelling or grammar

Ground rules

It is important to establish ground rules for your discussion group as this helps it to work well. Ground rules can cover issues such as: importance of acknowledging each other's messages, response times, methods of disagreeing, etc. Here is a set of ground rules agreed by one group of business and management students:

- Visit the online discussion group at least three times a week
- Keep messages short
- Be polite. No bad language or put downs
- Don't write and send a message if you are feeling emotionally upset
- Let people know if you are absent, e.g., due to ill health or a family problem.

Working together online

This involves carrying out your group task and you may be involved in exchanging information and ideas, writing materials together, making arrangements for face to face working. If you are debating and discussing different ideas then it is important to acknowledge other people's ideas ('I thought your idea was useful Sam . . .') and to put your views across without causing offence. Ways of doing this include starting your sentences with phrases such as: 'In my humble opinion (often abbreviated to IMHO)' or 'Perhaps we could also think about . . .'

In an online environment you need to be very sensitive to the feelings of others as there are no visual cues as to how someone is responding to your comments. In a face to face meeting we use nonverbal aspects of communication as a means of gauging what is happening and how someone is responding to a particular situation. In addition, it is much easier in a face to face situation to flexibly adapt our communications, e.g. by changing a sentence as we are part way through speaking it, than it is in a virtual environment, where once the 'send' key has been pressed, the message cannot be easily recalled. Consequently, it is advisable to always pause and review the contents of a message before you send it. If you are feeling very emotionally upset then it is often best not to send the message until you have reviewed it the following day. Indeed, if you are working in an online group and you experience differences of opinion or conflict it is often easiest and quickest to sort the issues out face to face where there is less likely to be misunderstandings. Face to face and even telephone conversations are often a much better approach to communicating with each other in a tricky situation.

Sometimes an online discussion becomes confusing as there are lots of messages and it is difficult to see where the group has got to. In this situation it is helpful if someone writes a brief summary and posts it up in the discussion group. In some online groups members will take it in turn (e.g., on a weekly basis) to summarize the current status of the group and its activities.

Online conferences or chat sessions

At different times during a course or module your tutor or group may decide to organize an online conference. This will enable you all to be involved in a real time (synchronous) communication process, in other words everyone involved in the online conference or chat session is online at the same time. This means that you need to be logged onto the appropriate part of the online site at the time that you have set for your chat session. At the start of the session introduce yourself (if necessary) and then get going with the chat session. Chatting with two or three people is relatively simple. If there are four or more people online then it is worthwhile asking someone to act as facilitator or coordinator.

Handling difficult situations

As in face to face learning, difficult situations may arise within your online group. It is worthwhile being prepared for this possibility and developing a range of strategies for handling them. It is generally easiest to organize a face to face meeting or telephone conversation to sort difficult matters out, although this is not always possible, as you then have access to a wider range of nonverbal and verbal cues and you can adapt your approach to meet the needs of the others.

Table 4.2 provides guidance for managing situations that arise online.

Getting the most out of tutorials

Tutorials provide an opportunity for you to work one to one or in a small group (i.e., of up to three students) with a tutor. Typically a tutorial will last from 30 minutes to an hour. Tutorials provide a valuable opportunity to gain individual help and also to have your queries or problems dealt with by the tutor. The following list of tips will help you to get the most out of tutorials:

Table 4.2 Handling difficult online situations

Difficult situations	Strategy for handling the situation
Flaming (the online equivalent of road rage)	Keep your cool! Try to defuse the situation Talk to the others face-to-face
Quiet students or browsers (sometimes called 'lurkers')	Invite other students to join in by name Ask them for their opinion If they are not coming online then send them an email or text message and invite them to get involved
Online work fizzling out	Discuss it online or in a face to face meeting Remind other students about the assessment requirements for the course or module Negotiate and produce a new action plan Close the online group

- Be on time
- Be prepared by coming along with a list of questions
- If you are asked to prepare for the tutorial then make sure you have carried out this work in advance of your tutorial.

Most tutors enjoy tutorials and prefer to work with students who have actively participated in their module and completed all necessary reading.

Independent study

One of the defining features of higher education is that students are expected to work independently. This means that between scheduled sessions such as lectures or seminars you are expected to work by yourself or with other students. You may be involved in a wide range of independent study activities including:

- Search for and selecting appropriate information resources
- Reading set textbooks, chapters, articles or other resources
- Preparing for lectures, seminars or tutorials
- Completing nonassessed coursework
- Completing assessed coursework
- Working with other students on group work

- Preparing to lead seminars or make presentations
- Attending additional optional lectures or workshops.

Chapter 7 provides guidance on independent study activities associated with projects, independent studies or dissertations.

Experiential learning

Experiential learning is based on the idea that particular experiences form the basis of learning opportunities. This concept was explored in Chapter 3 and Figure 3.1 presents the learning cycle which shows how a particular action (or experience) forms the first step in the learning process. Experiential learning is commonly used in management education and development where activities and events in the workplace are often used by tutors or trainers as a source of material which is then reflected upon, leading to individual learning and improved practice.

Experiential learning is often used in undergraduate education as a means of enabling students to learn about themselves and the different ways in which people behave in organizations. For example, a group of students may be asked to produce a group presentation and then to reflect on the process of working together and producing the presentation. This is experiential learning in the sense that the experience of working together in a group provides the basis for learning about teamwork. The process of reflection is likely to involve reading and thinking about theories of teamwork and then linking them with the actual experience of teamwork.

Most business and management students will take part in some kind of experiential learning activity in their programme of study. Some students really enjoy this type of learning activity while others prefer different approaches to teaching and learning. If you are involved in an experiential learning exercise then it is important to:

- Understand the aims of the activity
- Understand the different stages involved in experiential learning. These are likely to include:
  - Briefing
  - The task or process which forms the focus for reflection
  - Reflection on the task
  - Writing up the activity
- Actively engage in the experiential learning task

- Discuss and reflect on the task or process in a professional manner. This involves:
  - Standing back from the task or process and thinking about what happened; what worked well; what could have been improved; the behaviour of all the participants; and the emotions that were present during the task
  - Reporting back in a nonjudgemental manner, e.g., 'I noticed that Sam did not help us build the tower' or 'Ivan kept reminding us to keep to time'
  - Being honest about your own feelings, e.g., 'I felt uncomfortable at the start of the task as I didn't know what to do' or 'I was pleased when John made his suggestion and I wished that I had supported his idea rather than keeping quiet'
  - Linking the experience to theory, e.g., in team building activities this might involve relating the experience to theories of team development or team roles
- Experiential learning is often used as the focus for assignments. If you are asked to write up your experience it is important to check the assignment instructions and follow them. This type of assignment often requires students to demonstrate:
  - Ability to reflect on a particular task or event
  - Critical thinking
  - Ability to link theory and practice
  - Self-knowledge.

Working on case studies

Case studies are often used in business and management education as they provide students with the opportunity to apply their knowledge and skills to either a real situation or one that has been designed especially for educational purposes. Case studies provide students with an opportunity to deal with complex situations and they often have a number of possible solutions with no right answer.

Case studies may be of varying lengths from 250 to 10,000 words long and they may be augmented by multimedia materials, for example, videoclips, podcasts, or sound recordings. Case studies are likely to contain the following information:

- A description of the real world context
- Background information, e.g., facts and figures, forms or reports from the case study organization
- Organizational policies and procedures
- Additional references
- Questions to consider.

Many academic textbooks are supported by websites that contain case studies. Many business and management lecturers use case studies and the following list will help you to get the most out of them:

- Identify the aims and learning outcomes of the case study
- Read the case study materials and identify key themes
- Remember that some case studies contain additional and irrelevant information as this helps you to practise identifying relevant information
- Remember that you may need to obtain some additional information to help you work on the case study
- Identify any additional materials that are relevant to the case study, e.g., lecture notes, theoretical ideas presented in textbooks or other sources
- Respond to the questions that have been posed in the case study.

Further information about the assessment of case studies is available in Chapter 6.

Inquiry based learning (IBL)

This term is used to describe a variety of learning and teaching methods that are student centred and may include problem based, project based and work based learning. Kahn and O'Rourke (2005) identify the characteristics of inquiry based learning as:

- Students tackle complex problems or scenario
- Students take charge of their learning process and decide on their lines of inquiry and their study methods
- Students use their existing knowledge and also identify their learning needs
- The IBL tasks encourage students to search for new ideas or evidence
- Students take responsibility for presenting their findings and also the supporting evidence and reasoning.

IBL is used in business and management education as it enables students to develop a range of transferable skills including research skills, information and ICT skills, team working, problem solving, critical thinking and reflection, and also self-management. Figure 4.1. provides an illustration of the cyclical nature of IBL and it is based on the work of Bruce and Davidson (1996).

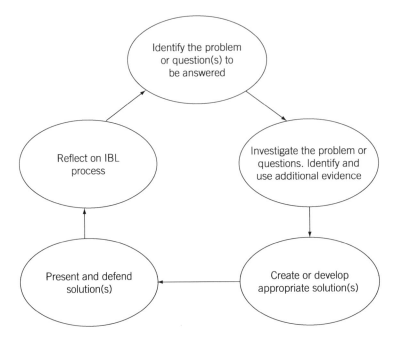

FIGURE 4.1 Inquiry based learning

Problem based learning (PBL)

Problem based learning (PBL), is a specific type of IBL, and it is extensively used as a means of enhancing student learning particularly about real life situations. PBL depends on the availability of realistic scenarios or problem situations that are then used as the focus for group work. The problem situation may be provided by the tutor or an employer, or a student may use a real life problem from their work experiences. The problem situations are typically complex and the students may be presented with a wide variety of data including irrelevant data. In addition they may be required to search for information using a variety of sources and/or generate their own data (e.g., from experiments or calculations). They are then required to create a possible solution or solutions to the problem and discuss this in their group, with their tutor or guest speaker. Finally, they are required to reflect on their problem solving process and their learning. In many respects, PBL attempts to imitate the types of complex situations that professional workers experience in their working lives.

Savin-Baden (2006) describes the process of PBL as involving the students or management practitioners in working through the following stages which involves both group and individual activities, and it may take place over a number of weeks or months.

Initial group activities:

- Study the problem
- Identify what you need to know to be able to solve the problem
- Identify the group learning needs
- Allocate the learning needs to individuals.

Individual activity:

- Research and achieve individual learning needs.

Group activities:

- Peer teaching of outcomes of individual research
- Reassessment of overall goals in light of outcomes of individual research and group discussions
- Formulating an action plan for managing or resolving the problem: this may result in the production of a specific output (e.g., proposal, fact sheet, presentation or report).

Another way of thinking about PBL is to imagine that the problem is at the centre of the learning process and that the students or practitioners develop their solution to the problem by accessing a variety of learning and information opportunities. Once they have resolved the problem, this is demonstrated by the students or practitioners producing an appropriate output (e.g., report or presentation). This output may form the basis of an assessment process. This process is illustrated in Figure 4.2. One aspect of the PBL process that isn't illustrated in this diagram is the communication processes, and students may use a variety of means including face to face meetings as well as online communications including tools such as email, discussion groups, chat rooms, wiki, mobile phones, message systems, etc.

Work based learning

In this section, the term 'work based learning' (WBL) is used to mean IBL where the focus is on working with and learning from a work based issue or problem.

Nowadays, some business and management students may be studying a WBL degree programme or modules in which the focus for learning is real life work based problems or issues. It is commonly used as a focus for management

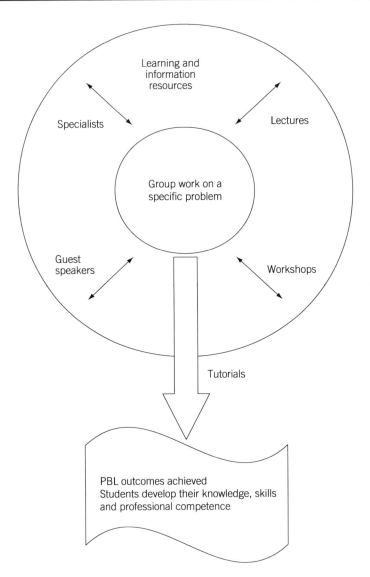

FIGURE 4.2 Problem based learning (originally published in Allan 2007)

education or continuous professional development as it enables individuals to
work with real problems that are relevant to them and their work.

Action learning

The concept of action learning was developed from the work of Revans (1980)
and it is commonly associated with management education and development
(Pedler *et al.* 2001). It involves a small group of people coming together and
working on a specific 'live' problem or issue; action learning emphasizes the
importance of experience and action. Figure 4.3 provides an overview of the
action learning process.

Action learning is a process that is frequently used for working on real life,
complex and 'messy' problems, and it is used as a way of helping practising
managers or directors to work on real life problems. An important part of action
learning is reflection, and a small, dedicated group working together using a
mixture of face to face and online communication tools accelerates this reflective
process. The stages in action learning include:

- Forming an action learning set of 6–8 members
- Deciding whether or not to have a facilitator; if the set decides to have a
  facilitator then this may be a group member or an external facilitator
- Deciding how often to meet and how to communicate with each other, e.g.,
  face to face and/or online using email, discussion groups and/or computer
  conferencing
- Reaching agreement on the problem(s) to be tackled
- Working on the problem(s) within the learning set including reflection in
  action and reflection on action (see earlier in this chapter)
- Developing solution(s)
- Reflecting on the whole process and its outcomes.

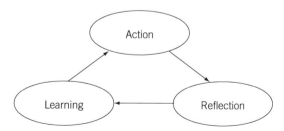

FIGURE 4.3 Action learning process

The advantages of action learning are that it enables individuals to share their expertise and gain different perspectives on the particular problem or context. In addition, individuals are likely to learn new approaches to problem solving and also develop their ability to reflect. However, there are some disadvantages to action learning as it is quite a time consuming process: it is normally limited to problems that have a medium or long term solution. In addition, the whole process depends on the skill of the tutor and the capabilities of the members of the action learning set. Action learning is sometimes used on management programmes and it enables students to learn the process of action learning – which is very relevant to working as a manager – as well as helping them to understand and develop solutions to management problems. Students who are employed as managers or team leaders while they study a part time business and management programme may find that action learning is used as a tool to enhance their subject knowledge, link theory to practice and improve their workplace practices.

Learning and developing using a learning journal

Reflection is a natural human activity and we tend to reflect on our daily activities, our successes and failures, our relationships and careers. This reflective process may take place during other activities – walking, swimming, showering, washing up. Reflection is important as it enables us to learn from our experiences – both our failures and successes. This helps us to improve our skills and practice. Some theoretical ideas about reflection are considered in Chapter 3.

The benefits of reflection include:

- Improved performance, for example in assignments
- Increased motivation and confidence
- Greater self-awareness
- Better understanding of the links between theory and practice
- Development of professional skills
- Development of career.

Learning journals are commonly used as a tool to encourage reflection and they are particularly common as part of a personal development process or on management development programmes. Reflective learners are people who think about their learning either as they are learning something or at the end of a learning activity (e.g., at the end of a lecture or seminar, or the end of a semester). Reflection is important as individuals who develop their ability to reflect are likely to become reflective managers who reflect on:

- Critical incidents or experiences
- Their strengths and weaknesses as managers
- How they can improve their management practices
- Their learning and development experiences.

Reflection is a very good tool for helping you to develop and improve both your academic and your professional practice. All it requires is a little time and a method of recording your thoughts such as using pen and paper, a laptop or a digital recorder. Different people will prefer to reflect in different ways. It is very important to record your thoughts and many students use a diary or exercise book to do so. Other students may type up their thoughts and some people like to tape record their thoughts. The important point is to keep a record of your reflective practice. There are many different ways of reflecting on your experiences and the following three examples are regularly used by students. It is worth noting that each of these methods concludes with the production of an action plan.

Reflection: example 1

The easiest way to start reflecting is to spend five minutes after a seminar or tutorial answering the following questions.

- What went well?
- What didn't go so well?
- What did you learn?
- What will you do differently next time?

The final question is vital as it enables you to identify and plan improvements to your approach. This process has been described in some detail in Activity 3.3, Developing your skills as a reflective student, in Chapter 3.

The following activity was completed by a business school student after an independent study session. She used the four questions and noted down her responses:

Example brief reflection activity

What went well?
Understood the key readings. Managed to find most of the references on the Internet. Made really good notes.

What didn't go so well?
I was tired and seemed to be struggling to stay awake at the end of the session.

What did you learn?
I can find my way around the Internet but perhaps could learn some short cuts. Using a colour coding system made it easier to make notes – they look good.

What will you do differently next time?
Time it better! Working in the evening after a full day of lectures was no fun. Next time I'll do this kind of session on a 'light' day.

Reflection: example 2

Critical incidents are those that often generate emotions or strong feelings. For example, you may be working on a group assignment and there are major problems between two students, you may obtain an unexpectedly low mark for an assignment, or you may find a piece of work very challenging. The following process may be used to reflect on a critical incident:

- Select a critical incident
- Briefly describe it
- What contributed to this situation?
- What was your role in creating this situation?
- What have you learnt from this experience?
- What do you need to do differently in future?

Reflection: example 3

Another useful source of reflection is your own personal response to a situation or process. The following questions may be used to reflect on your personal responses:

- How do you feel about this task, activity, group or module?
- What are you enjoying?
- What do you dislike?
- What do you need to do differently?

On some courses and modules you may be asked to keep a learning journal and this is a specific example of reflective practice. If you are asked to keep a learning journal as part of an assessment activity then you will be given guidance by your tutor. This topic is also covered in Chapters 2 and 6.

Summary

This chapter provides an overview of the many different approaches to learning and teaching in business and management education. It is important to understand these different approaches as this will help you to make the most of the different ways in which lecturers and tutors expect you to engage with your studies.

The chapter provides an outline of both tutor centred and student centred methods of teaching and learning. Common methods of teaching and learning in business and management education include lectures, seminars, e-learning, tutorials and independent study. Other methods that are widely used include experiential learning, case studies, inquiry based learning (including problem based learning and work based learning) and action learning. The chapter is completed with an introduction to the use of learning journals.

5

Finding and using business and management information

Introduction • The production and dissemination of knowledge • Searching and finding business and management information • Identifying and selecting relevant information • Academic reading skills • References and referencing • Summary

Introduction

The aim of this chapter is to help you to understand and use business and management information in your academic studies. Academic staff in universities carry out research and this is disseminated via publications. Understanding this process of knowledge production and dissemination will help you to understand the relative importance of different information sources.

Each year hundreds of thousands of books, journals and reports are published in the fields of business and management. An important skill that all students need to develop is that of searching and finding information using libraries and the Internet. Once you have found a number of items relevant to your work then you will need to evaluate and select relevant sources.

This chapter provides guidance on both searching for information and evaluating it. After selecting appropriate items then you will need to quickly read and assess their relevance to your studies. The section on academic reading skills provides guidance on obtaining the ideas and information that you require for your work. Finally, this chapter concludes with a section on referencing the work of others in your assignments.

The production and dissemination of knowledge

This section provides an outline of the processes involved in both creating and disseminating knowledge. One of the main functions of universities is to create and disseminate new knowledge through research. Your lecturers are likely to be involved in research activities as well as their teaching activities. Many lecturers work in research teams with colleagues from their own university, research institutions or from higher education institutions from around the world. Their research may be funded by the university, a government body, a private company or sponsor.

Figure 5.1 shows some of the characteristics of a typical research process. Research is normally carried out in teams and they will write up and then discuss their initial findings with colleagues. This often happens at conferences where a lecturer, who represents the research team, presents their findings for discussion and debate among the research community interested in that particular topic or theme. This is an important characteristic of the research process, i.e. it involves discussion and debate with peers. This process helps to ensure that the research meets the high standards required by the international research community. Once a research team has obtained feedback on their initial findings or ideas, then they will perhaps carry out more research and/or edit and amend their work to take on board the feedback. Finally, the research will be submitted for publication (e.g., as a formal report for the funder or as an academic article in a journal). Journal articles are normally peer reviewed before they are published. The process of peer review involves the journal editor sending the article to academic experts in the particular field. They will peer review the article (i.e., they will assess it and ensure that the researcher has produced a high quality piece of research). They will check the research methods and the claims of knowledge in the article. Once the editor is satisfied by the peer review process, that the article is well written and that it makes an original contribution to knowledge in that specific field then they will accept it for publication. This process enables knowledge developed as part of the research process to be disseminated to the wider academic community. It also highlights the importance of journal articles as a means of disseminating original research and new ideas. The peer review process ensures that journal articles (available in the library or through the library's e-resources) are of a high quality. This is the main reason that students are encouraged to use journal articles in their studies rather than items that they have identified via Google or Google Scholar, which are unlikely to have gone through a peer review process.

The last stage in the knowledge dissemination process occurs when the new knowledge is summarized and presented in forms that are likely to be used by business and management practitioners. Academic writing in journal articles is often rather abstract and difficult to read. Consequently, the main findings that are reported in journal articles are often rewritten in a more accessible manner and printed as:

- Articles in professional business and management magazines, e.g., *Personnel Today*, *The Economist* or *Accountancy Age*
- Articles in good quality newspapers, e.g., *Financial Times*
- Summaries in textbooks.

Textbooks are a particularly good starting point for finding information as they provide a framework of that particular field of knowledge and they identify key ideas and authors.

The knowledge process is summarized in Figure 5.2. It is interesting to note that, although a relatively small number of people may read the original academic article, large numbers of people may read a simplified version in, for example, professional journals or magazines. In addition, these sources are often used by trainers and human resource professionals as a means of keeping up to date.

Searching and finding business and management information

Successful students have often developed a good understanding of the framework of how information is organized in their subject area. You may develop your knowledge of the framework in your area by looking at the contents pages of standard textbooks and also by going into the library and seeing how books are organized on the shelves. Different libraries use different classification systems, and an easy way to get started is to search the online catalogue for a standard textbook. Once you find the classification code, which may be a mixture of letter and/or numbers depending on the classification scheme used by the library, then

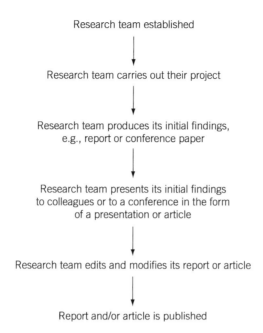

FIGURE 5.1 Overview of the research and knowledge production process

write it down. For example, the topic 'Economics of land' is likely to be found at the 333 using the Dewey decimal classification scheme and HD101 – HD1399 using the Library of Congress Scheme. Make sure that you write down the full code and you will then use it to find the specific item on the shelf. The classification code both describes the subject of the book and acts as a shelf location device. When you find the relevant shelf then you will be able to browse the books in your subject area and begin to build up a framework for the organization of the subject. One of the advantages of looking at books on the shelf is that you may serendipitously come across books that are of interest to you. It is important to realize that the books on your reading lists represent a miniscule amount of those published in that area. By using the library effectively you will be able to find a wide range of books including those that are readily available as they are not on reading lists.

During your time as a student, you will need to use a wide range of printed information sources including books, journals and reports, as well as electronic sources, including e-journals, databases and websites. As stated earlier, a good starting point is textbooks, which provide summaries and will identify key ideas and authors. You may also need to contact organizations or individuals for specific information. You may be quite experienced in using and navigating the

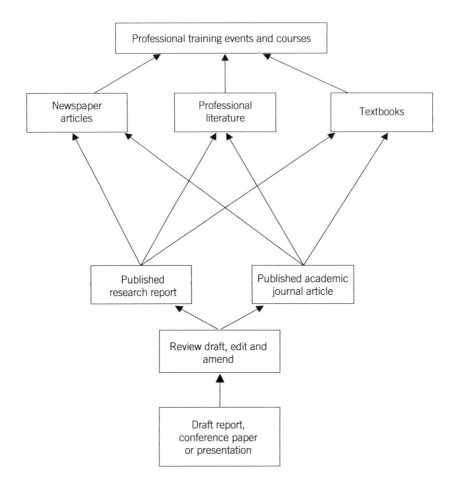

FIGURE 5.2 The knowledge dissemination process

Internet for general searching, but you will find that your university studies require you to develop advanced information skills so that you can identify and use reliable and credible academic information sources.

Many new university students think that they are effective Internet searchers because they can use Google or Google Scholar. However university level studies involve more skills than the ability to use Google, so you are advised to spend some time developing the more sophisticated Internet searching skills required for academic study.

In addition, you will need to develop skills in evaluating information sources so that you can answer questions such as:

- Is this source trustworthy?
- Is it reliable?
- Is it credible in the context of academic study and research?

Making the most of your library

Higher education library and information services are vast and they will provide you with access to an extensive range of resources and services, as shown in Table 5.1.

One of the most important resources is the library staff whose role includes helping students to make the best possible use of all their printed, electronic and multimedia resources. Making the most of your library involves:

- Making sure that you are enrolled in the library and have a library card. This often happens automatically at enrolment. Many libraries require students to have their library or student ID card with them in order to gain access
- Find your way around the library building(s). The best way to do this is to wander around and explore the library to:
  - Find out where the business and management books and journals are located
  - Find out where newspapers are kept
  - Discover whether or not there is a special reference collection with dictionaries and directories

Table 5.1 Typical library resources and services

Resources	Services
Academic journals	Cafe
Books	Computers including specialist equipment
Company data	for students with special needs
Dictionaries	Laminating
Directories	Meeting rooms for small group work
DVDs	Photocopying
e-Books	Quiet study facilities
e-Journals	
Financial data	
Image collections	
Legal information	
Reports	
Specialist collections	
Statistics	

- ○ Find out where the help desks are located. Find out if there is a special one aimed at business and management students
- ○ Discover the location of computers, photocopiers and other facilities
- ○ Find out where the quiet studies and the group study areas are located in the building
- ○ Finally, find out how you can borrow books and other items
- Find your way around the library website. The best way to do this is to explore the website to:
  - ○ Find out how to locate electronic books (e-books)
  - ○ Find out how to locate electronic journals (e-journals)
  - ○ Find out how to access guides to research, e.g., databases and indexing services
  - ○ Find out where the library help resources are such as:
    - □ Guides to the library
    - □ Guides to the e-books or e-journals
    - □ Guides to searching for information
    - □ Guides to specific information resources, e.g., reports, market research
    - □ Guides to referencing
- Asking for help from the library and information workers via email or library service points.

Finding and using different resources

As a student you will have access to an extensive range of information sources and it is worthwhile spending a little time becoming familiar with them. Table 5.2 summarizes the key features of common resources. Please note that this is a

Table 5.2 Different types of information resources

	Key features	How do you find them?
Books	Printed form Useful for providing an overview of the subject Include key ideas and research They will not contain the most up to date research	On the shelf books are normally organized by subject code (available on the library catalogue) To help find a particular book you will need to know the author's surname and initials, and the title
e-Books	Electronic version of printed form Useful for providing an overview of the subject Include key ideas and research They will not contain the most up to date research	Normally available via the library website. You may need a special user ID and password to access them off-campus Many e-books provide a wide range of facilities, e.g., bookmarks, notes facility, links to other resources

Academic journals: printed format and e-journals	These are available in a number of forms: printed, printed and e-journal, e-journals only Academic journals contain up to date research and also book reviews Journals are published in parts or issues and these come out several times a year Each issue will contain a number of articles and also some book reviews Peer review process helps to ensure that journal articles contain high quality research	To find a specific journal article you need to know: • The title of the journal, the year it was published and the volume and issue number • The name and initials of the author • The title of the article • The page numbers of the article (for printed version only)
Organizational websites	An important information source for many business and management students is organizational websites These will often provide a wide range of information about the organization Remember this information is likely to be biased in favour of the organization and its activities	Searching for organizational websites is very easy and they can be found using any search engine; some useful examples include: • Bank of England at www.bankofengland.co.uk • National Statistics UK at www.statistics.gov.uk • PriceWaterhouseCooper at www.pwc.com News and newspaper websites provide access to useful information too; useful examples include: • BBC at www.bbc.co.uk • *Financial Times* at www.ft.com • *The Times* at www.timesonline.co.uk
Individual weblogs	Individuals may have their own weblog in which they present their perspectives on the world; two examples include: • Dave Chaffey at www.davechaffey.com • Phil Bradley at www.philbradley.typepad.com/	There is no quality control of these sites so their content needs to be treated with suspicion However, there are many useful sites, e.g., individual lecturers, business librarians and independent consultants

short list and there are many more kinds of information resources in existence so it is worthwhile asking your librarian for help or obtaining a business and management information sources guide from the library.

A wide range of tools are available to help you find these different information resources and Table 5.3 provides a summary of those that are commonly used.

Table 5.3 Common search tools available from academic library websites

Search tool	Notes
Library catalogue	This will help you access a wide range of resources including books, journals, dictionaries, directories, abstracts and indexes Many library catalogues provide links to regional or national universities' catalogues. Your library website will be able to provide you with help in gaining access to these resources
Subject databases	Finding specific academic articles, company profiles or commercial reports would be an extremely time consuming process if you had to search through all the journals. Subject databases provide a quick and easy way to finding specific articles, company information or reports. These are normally available in electronic form via the library website. Common examples in business and management include: • Amadeus – company and financial information • Business Insights – business reports • Datastream – global market and financial information • Ebsco Business Source Complete – general business information including academic research, company profiles, market research reports, industry profiles • EcoWin – economic and financial data • Factiva – news and business publications • FAME – company and financial information • Financial Times – business and financial reports and analysis • ISTOR Business Collection – business journals • Mintel – market research reports • Web of Science – provides access to the Social Sciences Citation Index which enables you to track down research networks and connections To search for articles in indexes and abstracts use specific search terms or keywords, or author names. Different indexes and abstracts each cover a slightly different selection of journals and this means that you have to search a number of different indexes and abstracts in order to find all relevant articles Use the help facilities to improve your search

Using the Internet

The Internet is a source of two different kinds of information. First, it is used to distribute information that has previously been published in another source and this type of information is normally accessible using the types of information searching tools outlined in Table 5.3. Second, it is used to disseminate information that is only available on the Internet.

It is important to remember that anyone can put information on the Internet and that this information may be true or false and it may be inaccurate or out of date.

This contrasts with the type of information that you can access via your library as this will have gone through a number of checking processes (e.g., author, editor, publisher and librarian).

When you are searching for information for your academic studies you are always advised to use the specialist resources available via the library website. Many students limit their information searches by using search engines such as Google or Google Scholar. However, the usefulness of this type of search engine is extremely limited for university level academic work. One of the problems with using search engines is that although they will provide you with large numbers of references, you will waste a lot of time searching through them and evaluating their sources. It is much better to use a credible resource such as the subject databases accessible via the library website.

It does take some time to become familiar with the different subject databases and to learn how to use them. There are many online guides to the literature, and your university or college is likely to provide you with learning resources or tutorials to help you to find and use different business and management resources. In addition, many national libraries provide comprehensive tools, for example the British Library site at www.bl.uk provides useful information on business and management information.

There are many specialist tools aimed at students and useful starting points include:

- *Internet Business Manager* – a tutorial on Internet information skills for business management students www.vts.rdn.ac.uk/tutorial/business-manager
- *Internet Economist* – a tutorial on Internet information skills for economics students www.vts.rdn.ac.uk/tutorial/interneteconomist

Identifying and selecting relevant information

Use reading lists

The normal starting point for studying a topic is the reading list provided by your lecturer. Different lecturers will take different approaches to reading lists and these may include:

- Core textbook plus a list of recommended books, articles and websites
- A short reading list
- An extensive reading list
- No reading list – students are expected to find their own resources.

Talk to your lecturers and find out what their expectations are with respect to their reading lists. One common problem for students is that the recommended textbooks are not available in the library as they are out on loan. Books can normally be recalled from a reader by the library staff. Alternatively, if you search the library catalogue you are likely to find other books on the same topic that will contain all the required information.

Obtain up to date information

Textbooks rarely contain completely up to date information so you will need to update your knowledge by using information available in journal articles, reports in quality magazines or newspapers, and perhaps newly published books. Use the business databases (see Table 5.3 and your library website) to help you identify newly published articles. Up to date statistics are likely to be available from the relevant publishers.

Use reliable sources

One of the reasons that universities spend millions of pounds on their libraries is that this provides access to reliable resources and sources that have been approved by a professional librarian.

If you obtain resources that are accessible via the library, e.g., books, journals, business databases then you know that they will be reliable. Tables 5.2 and 5.3 provide you with guidance on some of the main resources.

If you access your resources using search tools such as Google or Google Scholar then they may be reliable or they may be worthless. Other sources such as many tabloid newspapers are not reliable and are best avoided in academic work.

Once you have identified your resources then you will need to evaluate them and the following checklist may be used to help you identify credible sources.

Checklist for evaluating information sources

Is it worth reading?

1 Is the author credible? For example, are they employed by a credible organ-ization? Are they qualified in the subject that they are writing about?
2 Is it a credible publication, e.g., accessible via the library system?
3 Is it a credible publisher? For example is the publisher a well known academic publisher?
4 Who has sponsored the research or publication? Is this likely to result in bias in the information?
5 How up to date is the information?

Does it contain good quality information?

6 What topics are covered? Are there any omissions?
7 Is the information accurate?
8 What evidence is it based on?
9 Is coverage of the material superficial or thorough?
10 Are the explanations and arguments logical and coherent?
11 Have any steps or discussion points been omitted?
12 Are there any other interpretations of this data?
13 What assumptions are made in this work?
14 Does the author identify the weaknesses in their work?
15 Does the information source repeat information available in other reputable sources?

Academic reading skills

Academic reading skills are different from leisure reading skills. Academic reading involves identifying new ideas, understanding different perspectives and devel-oping your understanding about a particular topic. Many students groan when they receive a reading list and wonder how they will ever read all the books on it. You don't normally need to read every book or indeed whole books. What you need to do is to identify and follow up key ideas.

There are different approaches to reading that will help you to read effectively and stay focused on your studies. It is worthwhile spending some time on devel-oping your academic reading skills as this will help you to get to grips with your subject and it will save you time.

Getting started with academic reading tasks

Once you have identified and selected relevant information sources then you need to think about why you are reading. There are three main reasons for academic reading:

- To explore and understand the subject in greater depth
- To obtain specific information
- To complete an assignment.

Reading techniques

There are a number of different approaches to reading:

- *Scanning* involves looking at the book or journal to decide whether or not it is relevant. Check the introduction, conclusions, contents pages, look at pictures and diagrams, and the index. This means you can quickly assess the content and decide whether or not it is relevant for your purpose
- *Skimming* enables you to identify specific information that may be useful to you. Skimming involves using the index to check the contents of the information sources and then surfing through specific sections or chapters
- *Deep reading* involves reading whole sections, chapters or a complete book, and is an active process. You may follow ideas by making notes or a Mind Map. If you can summarize key ideas or arguments in your own words you will know that you understand the topic. As you are reading you may be thinking about how your findings relate to a question raised in a tutorial session or in an assignment. If you are reading your own materials you may mark relevant passages with a highlighter pen or Post-it notes. Do not make any marks on library materials
- *Critical reading* involves evaluating the information source and criticizing it. You may want to compare it with the work of other authors, assess the methodology or criticize it in the light of your own experiences. Critical reading is time consuming and it is worth spending time developing this approach to reading – students who are critical readers often produce good quality assignments!

Working with journal articles

As you progress through your programme of study you will find that you rely less on textbooks and more on academic journal articles, which provide up to date research information. Earlier in this chapter, you were provided with guidance on searching for journal articles using business databases (see Tables 5.2 and 5.3).

Once you have found articles that appear relevant then you will find that they have the following structure:

- Title
- Author and author's affiliation
- Abstract
- Introduction
- Literature review
- Methodology
- Findings
- Discussion
- Conclusion
- Bibliography.

Working with academic journal articles is likely to involve the reading techniques discussed earlier in the following ways:

- *Scanning* the journal article is likely to involve quickly looking at the title and abstract and then flicking through the rest of the article to obtain a general sense of its layout and contents
- *Skim reading* journal articles is likely to involve reading the title, abstract, introduction and conclusions, and then glancing through the rest of the article. This will provide you with an overview of the article and its main findings
- *Deep reading* will involve working through the whole article and making notes. Some people find it helpful to do this on a photocopy of the original article, while other people keep their notes separate from the article. It is sometimes helpful to use diagrams, flowcharts, MindMaps or spider diagrams to help you make sense of the detailed arguments and information presented in the article. As a result of this process you should be able to identify the:
  ○ General research approach
  ○ Theoretical framework
  ○ Methodology
  ○ Research methods
  ○ Main points of argument
  ○ New knowledge created by the research
- *Critical reading* involves asking questions about the research and comparing it with other works in the same field. Table 5.4 provides a list of questions that you may use to critique the literature. Many of these questions relate to research methodology and this is covered in Chapter 6.

Table 5.4 Questions to ask when critically reading a journal article

Sections of an academic journal article	Questions
Introduction	What problem or issue does the research address? What are the research aims, hypotheses or questions? How does this research relate to previous research?
Literature review	Does it cover the main themes and topics? Does it cover the existing literature in this field? Is it up to date? Are there any major omissions, e.g., key references in this field?
Methodology	Did the author use an appropriate methodology? Is the methodology justified? Do other researchers in this field use this type of methodology? Is it clear how data has been collected and analysed? Is the sample size or number of respondents appropriate for this type of study? Were ethical issues addressed?
Results	Were the results clearly presented? Were the results interpreted correctly? Were any unusual or unexpected results explained? For quantitative studies: did the author consider issues of validity, reliability and generalizability? For qualitative studies: did the author consider issues of credibility, transferability, dependability and confirmability?
Discussion	Does the author link the findings to the original research aim, hypotheses or questions? Does the author link the results with the established literature in this field? Are the claims made by the author in line with the results? What new knowledge has been generated in this study? Has the author critiqued their own research approach, methodology and findings? Has the author identified new areas of research as a result of their work?
Conclusions	Do the conclusions follow on from the findings and discussion?
List of references	Are there any gaps? Are there any items that you will need to obtain and read to help you evaluate this article?

Strategies to help you develop your academic reading skills

The following strategies will help you develop your academic reading skills:

- *Be active*. Think about why you are reading and what you want to gain from the information source
- *Make notes or draw diagrams* to capture the main ideas in the work
- *Choose the right time to read*. You might find that you are more alert during the morning and that, by evening, your attention span is short. Read at times when you are most alert
- *Work in the right environment for you*, i.e., somewhere where you feel comfortable and alert
- *Reduce distractions*. Turn off the television and your mobile phone
- *Be selective*. Do not think that you should read everything in depth. Use the scan, skim, deep reading and critical reading techniques
- *Don't be afraid to experiment*. Pick a journal article and read it, adopting each of the techniques to demonstrate to yourself what can be achieved from each strategy. Experiment with different approaches to making notes
- *Use a wide range of sources*. Relevant sources may include: friends or members of staff; watching a relevant television programme; keeping up to date with current affairs information; printed books and journals; resources on the Internet; market research reports; company annual reports; etc.
- *Work with a friend* and share out the reading tasks. Select a chapter in a textbook or a journal article each and read it. Then present a summary to each other. Talking about the ideas that you read about will help you to understand and remember them.

Activity 5.1 Developing your academic reading skills

The purpose of this activity is to help you to develop your academic reading skills. Complete this activity after you have spent some time reading part of either a textbook or journal article. Please answer the following questions:

1 What went well? For example did you use any of the strategies to help you develop your academic reading skills that are described above?
2 What could be improved? How could you have gained more from your reading?
3 What have you learnt about your academic reading skills?
4 What will you do differently next time to help you improve your academic reading skills.

You may find it helpful to reflect on your answers to these questions and to perhaps discuss them with a friend, tutor or study advisor.

Making notes

Making notes is a skill that will help you to manage the information content of your programme of study. Making notes is something that you will do in many different situations: lectures, seminars, tutorials, reading a book or journal, or reading company websites. It is a very important practical skill and your notes will help you to:

- Identify and understand key ideas
- Learn key ideas and information
- Keep a record of information for future use
- Prepare for assignments or examinations.

Making good notes is about identifying and selecting relevant information. Think about why you are making notes:

- Do you want an overview of the subject?
- Do you want to record extremely detailed information?
- Will you be sharing your notes with a friend?
- Are you looking for a specific piece of information?

This is important as it will affect how you make notes. There are different ways of making notes. You can:

- List main headings and topics using keyword notes
- Draw a MindMap or spider diagram
- Copy out specific details, for example, a quotation from a book or factual information.

> Beware: Direct copying (verbatim) or close paraphrasing (putting into your own words but still closely following the structure and argument contained in the text) may lead to accusations of plagiarism in assessed work. Always keep notes of your sources, for example book details, so that you can reference them.

Useful hints for making notes:

- To help avoid unintentional plagiarism make notes in your own words. *Do not copy word for word* when making notes from books, journals or the Internet
- Try reading a relatively long section, *close the book or switch off the computer screen*

and then make the notes in your own words without looking at the original source. This checks your understanding and avoids the risk of plagiarism
- Use highlighter pens or a colour coding scheme to distinguish different sections of notes
- Notes should be concise, clear and consistent
- Review your notes
- File your notes – be organized; it is no good making notes only to discover two months later that you have lost them.

Activity 5.2 Developing your note making skills

The purpose of this activity is to help you to develop your note making skills. Complete this activity after you have spent some time making notes (e.g., in a lecture or from a textbook or journal article). Answer the following questions:

1 What went well? For example did you use any of the useful hints for making notes that are described above?
2 What could be improved? How could you have become more effective in making notes?
3 What have you learnt about your note making skills?
4 What will you do differently next time to help you improve your note making skills.

You may find it helpful to reflect on your answers to these questions and to perhaps discuss them with a friend, tutor or study advisor.

References and referencing

When you write your assignments, dissertation or independent study then it is important that you are clear about what you want to say and also that you are firmly locating your work within the established field of knowledge for the topic. This means that you need to read relevant textbooks, journal articles and other sources. You will need to compare and contrast your argument or findings with those of established authors. In this way, you will be able to integrate your work in the field of knowledge relevant to the specific subject. This will demonstrate to your tutor that you understand the topic and current ideas in the field (as demonstrated by you making reference to published academic research).

When you make reference to the work of others you will need to follow standard referencing practices. This is one of the crucial areas that any student – experienced or novice – must fully understand. All students need to understand the import-ance of referencing (i.e., acknowledging the sources such as books, journal articles, newspaper articles, reports you have used in your assessed work). It is important to reference your work as this:

- Gives your work academic credibility. Your references are rather like a 'kite mark' as they demonstrate that you have based your work on credible aca-demic sources that have been through a peer review process
- Is good manners and acknowledges the person whose work you have used
- Makes it clear which is your work and which is the work of another person
- Helps the reader to track down the original sources
- Demonstrates how your work links into your subject area
- Prevents accusations of stealing other people's ideas or words (plagiarism).

The basic idea is that you must state the sources of ideas and information in your assignments. This means that you must give credit to or acknowledge the original source or author whenever you:

- Use a word for word quotation from another source
- Paraphrase or use your own words to describe or summarize an idea that you have obtained from another source
- Use facts (e.g., statistical data) used by another source
- Use an image or diagram from another source.

If you are unsure whether the information that you have provided should be referenced or not it is better to provide one to be on the safe side. The con-sequences of providing too many references are far less severe than those of not providing them at all or providing a list full of omissions.

   If you do not acknowledge the work of others then it is a form of *theft* (stealing other people's work and passing it off as your own work). Failure to acknowledge the sources you have used in writing your assignment is likely to result in an allega-tion of plagiarism being made against you. Some examples of plagiarization are:

- Cutting and pasting information from the Internet
- Copying paragraphs from a textbook or website and changing only a few words or sentences
- Copying a diagram and changing a few words or the layout
- Copying the work of another student.

Plagiarism is treated very seriously by all universities. Many universities now use special plagiarism detecting software, such as Turnitin, to help them to identify student's work that is similar to the work of published authors or other students.

This specialist software helps to make plagiarism much easier to detect. The penalties are normally very serious ranging from a mark of zero for the plagiarized work through to the student having their programme of study terminated. In addition, if you have been found to have plagiarized then this information may be included in a reference to a prospective employer. Most employers would not want to employ a thief!

> If you have problems with completing your assignments and handing in your work on time then talk to your tutor or the administrative support office. Do not be tempted to rush your work and not reference your sources properly. The penalties for either intentional or unintentional plagiarism are often severe and much worse than handing work in late.

Using sources

When you are using other sources it is important to note down their details as this enables you to correctly reference the source of the ideas. The information that you need to record is the:

- Name and initials of all authors
- Full title including any subtitle of the work
- Year of its publication
- For journal articles you need the title of the journal, the number of the volume, the number of the issue and the relevant page numbers
- For books you need to record the edition (if relevant), the location (i.e. town and country) of the publisher, the name of the publisher and page numbers (e.g., of quotations)
- For a website you need the website address and the date you accessed the website.

Many students now use computer based bibliographic tools such as EndNote and RefWorks to help store and organize their references. If you have access to these tools then it is well worth investing the time required to use them. They help to save time in storing and presenting references and they help to make your work look extremely professional.

How to reference

Your assignments should acknowledge the sources of all the ideas and information contained in them as this indicates to the reader that you are using other people's ideas. There are many different approaches to referencing and you will find your university or college will prefer you to use one specific system. Examples include the Harvard System and the American Psychological Association (APA) system. The APA system is used as the basis for many referencing software systems. You will need to find out which system you have to use and spend a little time learning how to use it. *Your business school or department will provide you with details about their preferred system.* If you have any questions about the referencing system then ask your tutor or a librarian. Further information about different referencing systems is available in Neville, C. (2007) *The Complete Guide to Referencing and Avoiding Plagiarism.* Open University Press.

The following provides some guidance on using one system (the name/date system), which is one form of the Harvard system.

You will use the information that you recorded when you were using your information sources to provide a reference to their work in two places:

- The main text of your assignment
- The list of references at the end of your assignment.

The main text of your assignment

In your assessed work, you will make reference to the work of others – by referring to their ideas, relating their findings to your findings, or by using their data. When you use data, information or ideas from others, then in the main text of your assignment you will provide information about the author (i.e., surname, date and possibly the page numbers). It is important to avoid the sloppy practice of including a reference at the start or end of each paragraph. Instead, integrate their work into yours. Here are five examples that indicate how to refer to other people's work in your assignment.

1 *Paraphrasing or using your own words to outline another person's idea.* In this example the idea came from the work of McConnell and was published in 2002:

> McConnell (2002) suggests that co-operative group work enhances students' performance in comparison with situations where they are working in competitive teams or competing individually with one another.

If there is more than one author then it is presented as 'Smith and Jones (2007)'; if the author's surname is used in the normal text (as shown in the example above) then only the date is surrounded by brackets. It is acceptable to put the author and date at the end of a sentence and in this case the form is normally (McConnell 2002) or (Smith and Jones 2007)

2 *Using a quotation* (i.e., the same words as the original author). Only a few quotations should be used in an assignment and, ideally, they should be short quotations, e.g., up to 15 words. If you use too many quotations in an assignment then you may lose marks. The following example shows the use of quotation marks '. . .' and the inclusion of the page number which enables the reader to track down the exact page on which the original quote is located. In this example the date only follows the quotation because the author's name is already clearly given:

> David McConnell suggests, 'students in cooperative environments perform at a higher level than those working in competitive or individualistic environments'.
>
> (2002:19)

As this is a quotation the page number of the original source is provided after the date of publication. This page number is *not* repeated in the list of references

3 If you *refer to a specific fact* then you must reference the source of this information, as illustrated in the example that follows, so that the readers can check the fact for themselves. In this example the information comes from a government report published by the UK Department of Education and Employment (abbreviated to DfEE):

> Between 1979 and 1999, the number of women in employment has risen by 6% (DfEE 2000).

4 If you *use someone's ideas that are described in another book* then you need to make it clear where this information has come from. In the following example, the student hasn't read the work of Johnson and Johnson (1999) and doesn't want to mislead the reader, so it is made clear where the ideas of Johnson and Johnson have come from, i.e., the work of McConnell.

> McConnell (2002) describes the work of Johnson and Johnson (1999) who . . .

5 If you *use information from a website*, e.g., a company website, then you need to identify the author. This is often difficult and it is normal practice to refer to the organization that owns the website as shown in the following example:

> The BBC (2008) provides information on the programme *The Apprentice* and this projects a particular image of . . .

Common errors

Common referencing errors made by students include:

- Inserting the whole reference of the original source. This is extremely clumsy as it makes your text difficult to read, and as most student assignments have a specific word count then it wastes precious words
- Inserting a web address (e.g., www.bbc.co.uk) in the main text of the work. It is always the author's name or names, which may be an organization's name that is included in the text. It is wrong to include the web address
- Including author's initials in their text. Only the surname is required
- Omitting page numbers from quotations.

The list of references at the end of your assignment

The details of all the work you refer to in your assignment are then given in a list at the end of your written work. This list may be referred to as a list of references or included in a bibliography. You will need to find out the format preferred by your tutors and university or college.

The list of references (or bibliography) at the end of your work should be arranged in alphabetical order (by author or organization name) as this helps the reader to find the full reference for the work. They will then be able to obtain a copy of that work and read it for themselves.

A commonly asked question about the list of references relates to page numbers. You do not need to put a page reference for any particular detail or quotation in your list of references. However, when you give details for a chapter in a book (where each chapter is written by a different author), or an article in a journal or periodical, then you should give the page numbers of the first and last pages. In the examples below you will be able to see how to correctly reference books, articles in periodicals (i.e., any form of publication that comes out regularly, such as an academic journal, a professional magazine or a newspaper) and websites.

List of references: example 1 (relating to examples used earlier in this chapter)

BBC (2008) *Return of The Apprentice*. Available at: http://www.bbc.co.uk (accessed 31 Feb. 2008).
DfEE (2000) *Labour Market and Skill Trends*. London: HMSO.
McConnell, D. (2002) *Implementing Computer Supported Cooperative Learning*. London: Kogan Page.

List of references: example 2

Galliers, R. D. and Baker, B.S.H. (1995) Strategic information management, in T. Jackson (eds), *Cross-Cultural Management*. Oxford: Butterworth-Heinemann, pp. 143–72.

Handy, C. (1991) *The Age of Unreason*, 2nd edn. London: Arrow Books.

Keble, J. (1989) Management development through action learning, *Journal of Management Development*, 8(2): 77–80.

Nixon, B. and Pitts, G. (1991) W.H. Smith adopts a new approach to developing senior managers, *Industrial and Commercial Training*, 23(6): 3–10.

Nutt, P. (1984) Types of organisational decision processes, *Administrative Science Quarterly*, 29: 414–52.

Noakes, S. (1997) Consumer spice, *Logistics Manager*, Nov./Dec.: 6–7.

Nentwich, M. (1996) Opportunity structures for citizens' participation: the case of the European union, *European Integration online Papers* (*EioP*), no.1. Available at: http://eiop.or.at/eiop/texte/1996–001a htm (accessed 5 Nov. 1999).

Payne, R. and Pugh, D. S. (1971) Organisations as psychological environments, in Warr, P. B. (ed.), *Psychology at Work*. Harmondsworth: Penguin.

Peters, T. J. and Waterman, R. H. (1982) *In Search of Excellence*. London: Harper & Row.

Rowntree, D. (1996) Making open and distance learning work, *The Implementation of Open and Distance Learning*. Milton Keynes: Open University. Available at: http: //www-iet.open.ac.uk/pp/D.G.F. ROWNTREE/MBL.htm.MOADLW.htm (accessed 7 Apr. 1999).

Smith, F. (1994) Is there life on Mars? *The Telegraph*, 14 Mar. Available at: http: // www.telegraph.co.uk (accessed 8 Jun. 1995).

Some frequently asked questions about referencing

1 *How do I reference electronic journal articles?* Many journals and reports are now available from gateway services or business databases such as Business Source Premier. In this situation the web address alone is an insufficient reference, because it shows only the access mechanism used to get the material and does not properly identify the source of the ideas or the arguments. You will need to provide information about the source document:

> The name of the author (surname + initials); date i.e. year of publication; the title of the paper; the title of the journal and volume, issue and spread of pages over which the article is found; web address plus date accessed.

2 *What if I want to keep referring to the same text?* You will often be able to do so without repeating the same reference several times. Where you do need to repeat the reference, do repeat it. This is preferable to using the Latin *'ibid.'*, which used to be common practice

3 *What if I want to refer to two books by the same author?* If an author has written two books in the same year and you want to refer to each of them, then indicate the different texts using alphabet numbers, e.g., Smith (1997a) and Smith (1997b)

4 *How do I reference an email?* The appropriate format is:

> Smith, J. (JaneSmith@auniversity.ac.uk) (2005) Writing essays, 20 May. Emails to: Sheena Another (s.another@uni.ac.uk)

5 *How do I present a short quotation?* Place quotation marks ' ' around all words that are being quoted. You should also retain the particular punctuation, spelling or italics of the original. You must give as reference for your quotation the author's surname, year of publication and the page number(s). Place these details in the text in rounded brackets, e.g., '(Smith, 1987:15)'. You should not give the page numbers of a quotation in your list of references.

> 'Students in cooperative environments perform at a higher level than those working in competitive or individualistic environments'.
>
> (McConnell, 2002:19)

6 *How do I shorten a quotation?* If you do not want to include a full sentence from the source you are quoting, you can shorten a direct quotation by the use of omission marks (. . .). However, the quotation must still make sense in its short-ened form so it might be necessary to add an extra word or two to ensure it reads correctly. These extra words should be contained within square [   ] brackets

7 *What should I do if I want to quote something that contains something that is inaccurate, grammatically incorrect or misspelled?* Use the indication '[sic]' within a quotation if it contains a claim or phrase that you feel is incorrect, outdated or unacceptable, or a word or phrase that is grammatically incorrect. It should be inserted directly after the phrase to which it refers e.g.,

> Jane Smith said 'I got mad [sic] with the worker'.

8 *How do I set out quotations?* Always use quotation marks at the start and end of *all* in-text quotations. Short quotations (a few words only, less than one line of print) can be incorporated within the body of your argument. Make sure the sense flows properly between the quotation and surrounding text. Use quotation marks. Place the reference details at the end of the sentence in which the quotation occurs. For example:

Within the Gillette company, 'out of every forty-five carefully developed new product ideas, three make it into the development stage but only one eventually reaches the marketplace'.

(Armstrong and Kotler, 1999:263)

Longer quotations should be separated from the body of your assignment by a line space before and after the quotation. The quotation should be indented on either side, and the reference should appear in brackets on the line immediately below. Use single spacing for the quotation:

Dupont has found that it can take as many as three thousand raw ideas to produce just two winning commercial products, and pharmaceuticals companies may require six thousand to eight thousand starting ideas for every successful commercial new product.

(Armstrong and Kotler, 1999:263)

Continue your assignment using normal spacing. The full reference for the above quotations would appear in your list of references as:

Armstrong, G. and Kotler, P. (1999) *Marketing: An Introduction*, 5th edn. Upper Saddle River, NJ: Prentice Hall.

9 *How do I reference information from the Internet?* The Internet is a source of two different kinds of information: first, it is used to distribute information that has previously been published in another source; and, second, it is used to disseminate information that is only available on the Internet. It is very important that you take the trouble to find the proper reference for materials that have been obtained through the Internet. The first case (i.e., material that has been published elsewhere), is shown in the following two examples:

Nentwich, M. (1996) Opportunity structures for citizens' participation: the case of the European union, in *European Integration online Papers* (*EioP*), no.1. Available at: http://eiop.or.at/eiop/texte/1996–001a htm (accessed 5 Nov. 1999).

Smith, F. (1994) Is there life on Mars? *The Telegraph*, 14 Mar. Available at: http: //www.telegraph.co.uk (accessed 8 Jun. 1995).

In the second case (i.e., material that is only available on the Internet) then you will reference the material in the following manner:

BBC (2005) Healthy eating in schools. Available at: http://www.bbc.co.uk (accessed 3 Sept. 2005).

Summary

The aim of this chapter is to help you to understand and use business and management information in your academic studies. The chapter began with an overview of the academic knowledge production and dissemination process and highlighted the importance of academic journal articles. Finding and evaluating business and management information can be a time consuming process and you are advised to use the library resources, particularly business databases, as a means of finding credible information for use in your studies.

Once you have identified credible information sources then you will need to read them and assess their relevance to your work. Four reading techniques are presented (i.e., scanning, skimming, deep reading and critical reading); selecting the appropriate technique will help you obtain the ideas and information that you require for your work. Once you are working with the relevant materials then you will need to make notes and this chapter provides guidance on different note making strategies. Finally, this chapter concludes with a section on referencing and avoiding accusations of plagiarism in your assignments.

6

Assessment

Introduction • Examinations • Online assessment activities • Assignments • Presentations • Oral or viva voce *examinations • Portfolios • Learning journals • Plagiarism and other forms of cheating • Summary*

Introduction

The purpose of this chapter is to provide you with general guidance on the types of assessment activities that you may experience as a business and management student. Assessment is one of the most important aspects of your student experience and it gives you the opportunity to demonstrate to the examiners (and also to future employers) your knowledge and skills. Your final degree result will depend on your achievement over a whole series of assessment activities. If you understand the assessment process and how it is structured then this will help you to do well.

A wide range of assessment activities are used to assess students' achievement of the learning outcomes of individual courses or modules, and their degree programme. Each form of assessment has its own rules and it is important to understand them. If you are successful in one type of assessment activity, for example writing a traditional essay, this does not necessarily mean that you will be successful in other assessment activities, e.g., a workplace project. The more you understand the different forms of assessment and their own particular rules then the more likely it is that you will do well in all your assessment activities on all your modules or units of study. Common forms of assessment include:

- Examinations
- Online assessment activities

- Assignments – essays, reports or case studies
- Posters
- Presentations
- Oral exams or *viva voce* examinations
- Portfolios
- Learning journals.

Each of these topics is considered in turn in this chapter. This is followed by a section on plagiarism and referencing. This is a very important topic and you will find useful information on referencing in Chapter 5. In addition, assessment activities are covered in the following chapters: Chapter 7 covers projects, dissertations or independent studies; and assessed group work is the focus of Chapter 8.

Assessment is a hotly discussed topic by students and staff. This is because the results of the assessment process have a significant impact on your future life and so they are very important. If you are a new student and you have not completed assessed work for some time, perhaps because you have taken a career break to returned to education, then it is particularly important for you to get to know and understand the assessment system. In addition, if you are an international student and have little educational experience in the country where you are studying then it is important to learn how you must adapt your previous study strategies to enable you to be successful in your new educational environment. Understanding the assessment process and being prepared for it will help you to do well in your studies.

One particular aspect of the assessment process that sometimes causes confusion and may lead to disagreements between students and tutors relates to marking regimes. Different countries and different universities within a country will have their own approach to marking. For example, it is common practice in some countries, such as the USA, to use the whole range of marks from 0 to 100 percent, and marks may be clustered in the 60 to 100 percent band. In other countries such as the UK the marking range is also 0–100 percent but marks tend to be clustered between 40 and 80 percent. This means that a student who has studied in the USA may perceive a mark of 65 percent as a poor mark but in the UK system this is viewed as a very good mark. Another difference relates to how a student's achievements are described. In some countries, students receive a transcript which contains the final marks for each module or unit and an overall average for their programme of study. In the UK, students will receive a final degree result that is described as:

- 1st class honours (equivalent to an average mark of 70 percent or above)
- 2nd class division 1 (2:1) honours (equivalent to an average mark of 60–9 percent)

- 2nd class division 2 (2:2) honours (equivalent to an average mark of 50–9 percent)
- 3rd class honours (equivalent to an average mark of 40–9 percent)
- Ordinary degree (as a result of having achieved the required number of academic credit points to pass).

In addition, students in the UK will receive a transcript that details their modules of study and their results for each module. Consequently, it is worthwhile finding out how the marking system works in your business school or department.

Confusion sometimes arises as a result of different forms of assessment within a programme of study giving rise to different ranges of marks. For example, students who take exams in statistics, quantitative methods and some elements of accounting and finance, or economics may achieve marks in the range from 0 to 100 percent. This is because there is a 'right' and 'wrong' set of answers and if your answers are 100 percent correct then it is possible to achieve a mark of 100 percent. In contrast, it is much harder to achieve a mark higher than 80 percent in written assignments such as essays, case studies, workplace projects or dissertations. Again, it is worthwhile checking with your tutor to find out about the range of marks used for a particular form of assessment.

Common problems that arise during assessment processes are often caused by students:

- Leaving it to the last minute
- Misunderstanding or not following the assessment guidance, e.g., not answering the question; writing an essay that is too long or too short
- Accidentally or intentionally using unfair means, e.g., not referencing sources; cutting and pasting information from the Internet; cheating in exams (see also Chapter 5)
- Ignoring the instructions about the procedure for submitting work
- Submitting work late.

Examinations

Examinations are widely used as a means of assessing students' knowledge and skills. Examinations are normally time constrained meaning you are working against the clock, and they may be organized in a number of different ways including:

- Unseen examinations where you don't see the exam paper in advance

- Seen examinations where the exam paper, which may include a case study, is available to students in advance of the examination
- Open book examinations where you can take your notes or a textbook into the examination.

Examinations are an essential part of the assessment process. You will need to find out how your university or college organizes examinations and the ways in which information about examinations are provided by your department or business school. Ensure you know the value of the examination in the assessment process as this helps you to decide how much time and energy to invest in preparing for it. For example, does it count towards 10 or 50 percent of the total mark for the module or course. The exact date, time and location of the examinations will be posted on notice boards or circulated by email prior to the assessment period. It is your responsibility to ensure that you are fully aware of the examination arrangements.

If you have a disability that may affect your performance in examinations then contact your personal supervisor, tutor or the disability service as soon as possible and well before the start of the examination period. If during the assessment period, you experience something that is likely to affect your performance (e.g., ill health, personal problems or bereavement) then contact your personal supervisor, tutor or support office. You will be asked to complete a form and provide evidence of your situation and this will then be taken into account during the assessment process.

The following quotations describe the exam experiences of two students:

As a mature student the last exam I did was at 16. I haven't done an exam since I left school. I was terrified. The revision sessions were good and the tutor made us do a test question in exam conditions. This helped. On the day itself I was terrified. I hid around the corner from the exam room – I didn't want to see or talk to anyone. When I got in the exam room I found it hard to find the right desk but the tutor showed me where to go. Once I began writing my name and student number on the exam books I felt a bit better. When we were told to open the exam paper and start, my heart sank. I could hardly read the questions. I spotted one question that I could do and got going. After 10 minutes I began to relax. Somehow I got through the exam and managed to write for the full 2 hours. We went to the pub afterwards to celebrate. I was thrilled to get 52% for the exam. Next time, I'll do even better.

I like exams as I have a good memory. They are much less hassle than assignments and group work. I start revising a month before the exam and revise for 2–3 hours a day. Once in the exam I do notes on each question that I'm going to answer. I then answer them. My advice to other students is to get organised and put the time in. Tutor revision sessions are useful.

Revision

The aim of the examination process is to test your knowledge and understanding in an environment with a time constraint. Examinations test your memory skills, your understanding of the subject and your ability to apply knowledge and skills to a specific situation. They also seek to evaluate some generic skills such as time management (have you answered all the questions you need to in the given time period?) and your ability to perform under pressure. These are skills that everyone needs in working life.

Students who are successful in the examination process are those who have developed an effective preparation technique and who are also able to manage themselves and their time during the examination.

Some students prefer to plan and begin their revision well in advance of the examination date, for example by studying specific topics throughout the semester and at a time when their schedule is less pressurized. Some prefer to revise during the weeks before the examination while others prefer to leave revision until the last minute when there is little chance that they will forget what they have revised. Conventional wisdom is that revision over a period of time is more effective then last minute cramming. However, you should work according to what suits you best. You may want to explore and experiment with different approaches so that you know which approach suits you best.

It is during revision for an examination that you are likely to realize the importance of making good, well referenced notes both during and after your lectures and seminars. Time invested in making notes will mean that you are well prepared for the revision process. If you have clear, well organized and easy to read notes you will find your revision easier than if your notes are badly labeled, disorganized and difficult to read.

It is useful to look at some of the recent past examination papers for each of your subject areas. This will help you to understand the structure of the exam and also the type of questions that may come up and the language used in examination questions. However, be aware that exams do change over time so ask your tutor if past examination papers are likely to help you in your revision. It is important that you know in advance the structure of your examinations. Look at an examination paper and become familiar with the structure of the paper. As you are looking at the paper, answer the following questions:

- Is it divided into parts?
- How many questions should I answer?
- Are there any mandatory questions?
- What is the format of the questions, e.g., multiple choice, short answer, calculations, essay style answers?
- How much time is there to complete the exam?
- How should the time be divided up between the different parts and questions?

A common error made in exams is that a student doesn't understand the structure of the exam paper and then fails the exam as they didn't follow the instructions. If you are in an examination and you are not clear about the instructions then ask the invigilator for clarification. Examples of past papers are normally available via your university or college website or virtual learning environment.

Most students prepare a revision schedule and work out the times that they can commit to revision. Remember to be realistic. You will have other activities during this time, for example, lectures and seminars, assignments or part time work. Remember to work on all the modules or courses that are going to be assessed. Do not put all your energy into revising for one module or course at the cost of others. One common error made by some students is that they spend too much time planning their revision and drawing up beautiful timetables rather than actually doing the work!

Allow yourself some relaxation time during your revision – you will perform better if you have some breaks from your revision, where you spend time with friends or give yourself time to have a coffee or go for a walk. The end result of six hours' nonstop revision is likely to be less productive than four sessions of one-and-a-half hours, with an hour's break in between each session.

Attend revision sessions organized by your tutor as this often provides valuable insights into the examination, your tutor being the person who will be marking your examination script. Revision sessions are important as they provide a means of obtaining additional help and also identifying those topics that the tutor highlights. These sessions also provide you with an opportunity to ask questions either about the subject or the examination itself.

There are several ways in which you could revise: some students work better alone, preferring peace and quiet; other students prefer to work with one friend or a whole group. If you prefer to revise on your own then it is always useful to spend a little time discussing the subject matter with a friend to ensure that you have grasped the key ideas or points. Talking is a useful way of clarifying your understanding. The choice is yours – remember to use an approach that works for you.

Once you have carried out some revision, you may find it useful to practice answering typical examination questions. Many people find it helpful to write outline answers in response to sample questions. If you are working with a group of people then you may want to exchange and 'mark' each other's answers.

Sitting examinations

Before the exam

- Have an early night so that you feel bright and refreshed. Don't party the night before an exam. If you have problems waking up then use an alarm clock and ask a reliable friend to phone you
- Have some breakfast (or lunch) before the exam as it is hard to concentrate if you are hungry
- Make sure that you know the correct date, time and place of the examination
- If you do not know the location of the examination then find out and visit it in advance of the exam
- Allow plenty of time to travel to the exam venue; get there early
- Make sure that you have the correct equipment with you. Check the examination instructions about what is allowed or not allowed in the exam room. You are likely to need your student identity card
- International students are sometimes permitted to use a language dictionary unless it is expressly forbidden in the examination paper's instructions. However, students' own dictionaries will be checked during the examination for notes and annotations, so make sure you use a 'clean' copy otherwise you may be accused of cheating.

At the start of the exam

- Complete the examination paperwork with your personal details
- Look at the examination paperwork and read the instructions
- Quickly skim through the examination paper
- Read and analyse the questions. Think about every word in the question and consider what the examiner requires. Table 6.1 provides guidance on the language used in exams and assignments
- Some people find it helpful to make a list of the main points they intend to cover for each answer
- Start writing. Many people find it best to start with the 'easy' questions.

During the exam

- Try to write clearly so that the examiners can read your work

- Keep an eye on the clock. Divide your time up so that the amount of time you spend on each question is proportional to the marks that are allocated to each question
- If you are running out of time, structure your response in note form or bullet points – writing anything is better than nothing
- Give yourself a minute or two to rest in between answers. This time may be used to gather your thoughts and also relax your eyes and writing hand
- Allow 5 minutes at the end of the examination to read through your answers, correcting any mistakes, and add any final details
- Cross out any rough notes that you made during the exam by putting a line through them. This will mean that your rough notes are not marked by the examiner.

Useful tips for doing well in exams

Most tutors have large numbers of examination papers to mark in very short time periods. If you make the marker's task easier by structuring your question in a logical way and using headings and subheadings then it is likely to be to your benefit. Make sure that your writing is legible. In addition, if you include some interesting examples or references that other students are unlikely to use this will help to make the tutor's task more interesting, and your work will stand out. You will also demonstrate that you have read widely around the subject, which may help you gain some additional marks.

What to do if you panic

- Throughout the examination remain calm. Keep your focus on the questions and your answers. Start with the easier questions. Concentrate on what you *can* do rather than what you cannot
- If you do start to panic, put your pen down, shut your eyes for a few moments, take some deep breaths and then start writing again
- If your mind goes blank then start to write – either write whatever you know about the topic or write about how you are feeling. This often helps people to get going again. Once your mind clicks into action then cross out this writing and get started on the examination answers again
- If you feel really stuck then ask to go to the toilet. Sometimes the act of walking around will help get your ideas flowing again.

Cheating in exams

All universities and colleges have good systems in place to catch cheats. Cheating during an exam means using unfair methods to gain an advantage over other students. Your university or college will have a code of practice about the use of unfair methods and will list the types of materials that are prohibited in an exam. Cheating outside of the exam is also obviously prohibited, for example arranging for a friend to sit the exam for you or attempting to get hold of an unseen exam paper before the exam. The penalties for cheating are high and each year students are expelled from university or college because they are caught cheating. This has a long term impact on their career as, if asked to provide a reference, the university or college will mention the expulsion and the reasons for it.

Prohibited materials in examinations often include:

- Mobile phones
- Some types of calculator
- Revision notes
- Revision planners
- Prepared quotations
- Written out equations
- Pre-prepared essay structures
- Dictionaries that have notes or annotations contained within the pages.

It can be an offence even to have these materials on your person, or on or near your desk – even if you have not used them. Therefore, you are strongly advised not to take them into the examination room. If you have any notes with you that you have been using for last minute revision then either leave them in a coat pocket at the back of the room, throw them away before you enter the hall, or give them to an invigilator before the examination starts. The penalties for being caught with prohibited material (even if you have not used it) or cheating in any way are very severe.

Students who do well in examinations are those who have developed effective revision techniques and know their subject. They also follow the instructions in the examination papers and answer the set questions rather than questions that they hoped would be set! It is a good idea to take up all the assistance and support given by your department or business school. A useful additional source on exams is: Levin, P. (2004) *Sail Through Exams!* Buckingham: Open University Press.

Online assessment activities

Online tests are now a very popular method of testing students' knowledge. Most online tests use multiple choice questions in which you have to select the correct answer from a list of possible answers. The possible answers need to be analysed carefully. One of the advantages of this form of assessment is that you don't need to write long essays. In addition, it is sometimes possible to deduce the correct answer by carefully working through the different options. However, you will need to have detailed subject knowledge to do well in this type of exam. If your programme of study involves online tests then it is likely that you will be first given a practice test. It is important to make use of this opportunity as it gives you the chance to become experienced with both the online test system as well as the test itself.

Online tests may be taken in a computer room and this type of test is very similar to traditional exams. In particular, tutors or invigilators will be able to provide you with assistance if you have difficulties using the computer system.

Another common approach to online tests is to enable students take the test within a particular time frame (e.g., 48 hours). This means that you will be able to treat the online test as an open book exam. In this type of exam, individual students will receive a random set of questions from a question database and this helps to prevent students from copying each other's answers. A common problem with this type of test is that students often leave it to the last minute and if it is 11.59 pm there is unlikely to be help available from staff if you have problems with the system. The best advice is to give yourself plenty of time to do the online test.

Assignments

One of the commonest approaches to assessing student's knowledge is through written assignments, such as essays, reports or case studies. The ability to write clear and logical assignments or reports is an essential academic skill and it is also an essential professional skill. Individuals who can present well written reports containing ideas that are clearly backed up by evidence are able to influence the thinking of their colleagues.

Written assignments are a very common method of assessment as they provide your tutors with an opportunity to assess your knowledge and understanding of a particular subject area. Written assignments will cover all or some of the learning outcomes of a module.

Writing assignments

The following general guidelines may be used for carrying out any piece of assessed work and they are particularly relevant for writing reports, essays or case studies. If you are writing a dissertation or workplace project then see also Chapter 7.

Analyse the task

Before you start any piece of written work you should ask yourself the following questions:

- What is the purpose of the assignment?
- What do I need to demonstrate in this assignment?
- Who is my reader?
- What are my aims?
- Which form of writing will best accomplish these aims?
- What structure will best suit the purpose and aims of this piece of writing?

The main factors that will determine what mark you receive for a piece of written work will be:

- Did you actually answer the question?
- Did you demonstrate the relevant subject knowledge?
- Did you demonstrate that you understand the subject and take a critical stance to it?
- Did you demonstrate your academic writing skills?
- Did you demonstrate your research skills by using appropriate academic references in your work?
- Did you demonstrate correct grammar and spelling?

Assignments that receive a poor mark often demonstrate the following characteristics:

- Lacking an introduction and conclusion
- Lacking a logical structure
- Not answering the question set by the tutor
- Badly researched
- Containing too much or too little information about a particular topic or topics
- Lacking focus
- Not providing supporting evidence or examples
- Containing poor grammar and spelling
- Lacking references or incorrect references
- Not satisfying the required word limit.

It is worthwhile spending time analysing the assessment question(s) in an assignment, an examination or a presentation. Do not glance at a question then rush off trying to locate vast amounts of information without having a clear understanding of what is being asked of you. The best strategy is to:

- Spend time identifying the key words in the question
- Look at the verbs in the question as these will indicate both what the content of your answer should be, and the process or method you should adopt to provide that information. Highlight them
- Spend time thinking about exactly what is being asked of you. Table 6.1 provides explanations for some of the verbs that are frequently used by tutors in assessment questions.

Working on your assignment

It is important to leave sufficient time to work on your assignment. Leaving it to the last minute is likely to result in a low mark. Working on assignments involves a number of stages:

- Planning your assignment
- Identifying and using a range of information sources
- Identifying key ideas and supporting evidence
- Writing your first draft
- Reviewing your work
- Editing your work
- Handing in your work
- Using feedback from assignments.

The first step is to plan your assignment and work out a general structure or framework for your work. Some students prefer to write out a list of headings and subheadings while others prefer to produce a diagram, for example, a MindMap or spider diagram. Some people use Post-its to identify and then organize their ideas. This provides an overview or framework of your assignment and you may find that you need to make changes as you work on the assignment.

Next you will need to identify, select and use a range of academic information sources (see Chapter 5). Remember to allow time for this step. You may need to recall items from the library or obtain them from a range of different sources and this may take a number of days or weeks. Once you have worked through the information sources you will need to identify key ideas and also supporting evidence. Make notes and keep a record of all relevant information sources as this will help you to write up your references.

The next step is writing your first draft. This involves working with your general

Table 6.1 Language used in assessment tasks (original source unknown)

Verb	Explanation
Account for	Explain or give reasons for
Analyse	Examine the topic, break up into parts and then examine the subtopics
Assess	Compare or judge the topic or situation. Weigh it up, e.g., the advantages and disadvantages, successful and unsuccessful features, important or unimportant characteristics
Comment on	Give your own point of view or those of researchers in the field with supporting evidence
Compare	Consider what are the similarities and differences
Consider	Weigh up the advantages and disadvantages or arguments for and against
Contrast	Consider both similarities and differences, and highlight the differences
Criticise	Make a judgement and use evidence to support it
Define	Give a brief definition or statement of the meaning of the topic
Demonstrate	Show or illustrate using examples
Describe	Give a detailed account of the topic
Differentiate	Explain the differences using examples
Distinguish	Explain the differences using examples
Discuss	Explore a topic from a number of different points of view and give evidence to support the different viewpoints
Evaluate	Weigh up or give your judgement about the topic. Judging the strengths and weaknesses of an argument and support your comments with evidence
Examine	This is very similar to analysing and involves exploring the topic in detail
Explain	Provide reasons that will account for the issue or example under consideration
Explore	Work through the topic and look at it from different points of view
Illustrate	Give examples
Interpret	Explain the situation or case study
Justify	Give reasons or evidence to support an argument or action
Outline	Provide an overview of the main points or issues
Relate	Show the relationships or connections between themes or topics
Review	Summarize the topic and current issues or themes
Summarize	Produce a brief account of the main points

structure or framework and starting to write notes under each topic. It is often best to leave writing the introduction and conclusion until the end.

There are two styles of academic writing used in business and management education. The traditional approach involves using a serious and formal impersonal tone. It involves presenting different ideas and the evidence to support them. This means not writing in the first person (not using 'my', 'I', 'we') and presenting an objective and depersonalized approach. In some subjects, for example some management topics, and also with assignments that involve reflection it is acceptable to use the first person ('my', 'I' or 'we'). If you are unsure which style to use then ask your tutor.

   The first completed draft of an assignment will never be good enough to submit. It is important to review your work and to check the content making sure that:

- You have met the assessment requirements
- Your introduction clearly introduces your work and also the topic
- The ideas are presented in a logical order
- The ideas are supported by evidence
- Your conclusions follow on from the ideas and evidence that you have presented
- Your work is based on a good range of relevant and up to date references.

If time permits, it is a good idea to leave a piece of work for a day or two and then come back to it. This will help you to see ways to improve the work. Alternatively ask a friend to look at it and give you feedback. You may find that you need to rewrite parts of your work. You may see that you have skimmed over an important topic and that you need to do some more research to provide a well balanced account. Time spent reviewing your work is likely to earn you additional marks as it will improve the quality of the final assignment.

   Editing involves checking the presentation of your assignment. Remember to double check any assignment requirements provided for you by your tutor. If you are writing a dissertation it is important that you double check the presentation requirements given in your handbook. Whatever your assignment, you will need to make sure that:

- The whole assignment is clearly written
- It includes a title, date and personal information, e.g., your student identification number
- You have met the word count requirements
- Any headings and subheadings that you have used are meaningful and consistent
- The grammar is correct
- The spelling is correct
- The references are correct.

It is best to edit your work at least twice, as this will help you to identify different areas for improvement.

Once you have completed your assignment, you will need to hand it in before the deadline. Most business and management departments or schools have very strict rules about handing in your work. Failure to follow these rules may mean that you lose marks, and it could even mean that you get 'zero' for your work. So it is vital for you to check that you understand the hand in procedures and allow yourself plenty of time to complete them correctly.

Plagiarism detection software, such as Turnitin, is now commonly used by many universities and colleges and you may be required to submit your work to an online site. If this is the case, you will be given instructions on how to submit your work. The first time you use the system allow yourself plenty of time to learn how to use it so that you can submit your work correctly. At peak submission times you may find that it takes several hours to use the system so do allow yourself time for delays. It is extremely annoying to produce a good quality assignment and then to have your mark reduced as you have not submitted it correctly.

After your assignment has been assessed you will receive feedback in the form of a mark or grade, and written feedback notes from your tutor. You should read carefully the feedback you receive on your assignment. Your tutor will provide guidance on the strong points of your work and also areas where it could be improved. If you find the feedback difficult to read, for example because it has been handwritten, or if you don't understand it then ask your tutor for clarification. You can use the suggestions for improvement as a means of gaining a better mark in your next assignment.

Essays

A well organized and easy to read essay is likely to consist of the following components:

- The introduction should introduce the reader to your essay and state its purpose and how you intend to answer the question. The introduction should also provide a brief outline of the main themes and why you have chosen the approach you did. It may also identify topics not covered in the essay. It is often easier to write the introduction last
- The main body of the essay forms the substance of a piece of work. It will present your arguments with supporting evidence that you have prepared in response to the question that was set
- Ensure that each paragraph makes a specific point and support this with evidence, examples or discussion. Make sure that it relates to your essay title. Your essay must flow from one paragraph to another and use linking phrases to provide continuity between the paragraphs, for example:
  - There are three advantages . . .

- ○ In the next paragraph, I will demonstrate . . .
- ○ This clearly supports the argument that . . .
- ○ To summarize this section, the main arguments in favour of . . .
- ○ I will focus my analysis on the views of three researchers . . .
- ○ I will now move onto the next topic . . .
- Make sure that you answer the question and stick to the main point or theme
- It is a good idea to include a few short quotations to support your findings and these also demonstrate your use of different information sources (see Chapter 5 for information on how to present quotations). However, don't over do the use of quotations. Remember that you are being marked on your understanding of the topic not the words of someone else
- Provide relevant examples that illustrate the points you make. This helps to make your work interesting to read and it demonstrates that you understand the subject
- Remember to reference all the information that you use in your essay (see Chapter 5)
- The conclusion should provide a summary of the key ideas or issues, and your concluding thoughts that either answer or respond to the main question. Your conclusion should not include new ideas or evidence
- You need to provide a list of all the references mentioned in your work. See Chapter 5.

An important feature of essays is that they are not normally divided into sections using headings or subheadings. Instead they are divided into sections through the use of paragraphs as described above. In contrast, headings and sub-headings are used to structure reports as described in the next section. However, it is worthwhile checking this point out with your tutor: do they expect to see headings and subheadings in an essay or will they mark you down for using them? Practices vary in different business schools and departments, and also from tutor to tutor.

A useful source on essay writing is Levin, P. (2004) *Write Great Essays!* Buckingham: Open University Press.

Writing reports

Report writing is a key skill that you need to develop as you are likely to be asked to write reports when you work for a business or other organization. A report is a formal and structured document normally used to present factual findings following some specific research. Reports tend to have a standard format. However different companies or academic departments use different formats, so make sure that you find out what is expected of you before you start your report. Below are two example formats: short report format and the long report format:

Short report format

This format is useful for relatively short pieces of work (e.g., up to 3000 words long).

- Title
- Summary
- Contents page (if appropriate)
- Introduction (introduces topic, context, scope, audience)
- Methodology (if appropriate)
- Theme 1 (presents the first theme or topic using an appropriate heading)
- Theme 2 (presents the second theme or topic using an appropriate heading)
- Theme 3 (presents the third theme or topic using an appropriate heading)
- Discussion (interpretation or analysis of your findings)
- Recommendations (if appropriate)
- Conclusions
- List of references
- Appendix (if appropriate).

Long report format

This type of format is used for reports in many businesses and organizations. The following is an example of typical report headings, but it is worthwhile checking the requirements of your tutor or organization:

- Title
- Abstract/summary
- Contents
- Executive summary (a brief summary of the report, e.g., a single page of A4, aimed at busy executives). In many business organizations this is the only part of the report that will be read by senior managers. It is vital that it contains all the essential information and ideas that you want to put across
- Terms of reference / Introduction (statement of what you were asked to investigate; by whom; your objectives; time period covered by the report)
- Procedure or research methods (what you did to gather facts; sources of information used; methodology of research)
- Findings/results (report your findings but do not discuss them – use graphs, etc., if necessary)
- Discussions (interpretation or analysis of your findings)
- Conclusions/recommendations (the main points for consideration drawn from your findings, do your findings prove or disprove your hypothesis?)
- Date and signature

- Appendix
- List of references.

Report writing is an essential skill for anyone involved in working in organizations. Many managers spend much of their time writing and also reading reports. This means that it is worthwhile investing time as a student in developing this skill. When you are working in an organization you will find that they have an inhouse style for structuring and writing reports and you will need to learn how to follow this style. One important difference between writing a report at university and at work is that at university you will be writing for your tutor or tutors and this means that you know your audience. In contrast, when you are writing a report at work, the report may be circulated widely and may be read by people who you had not envisaged as your primary audience. This means that it is important that you provide the background and context for the report, and make it as clear as possible. If necessary, additional supporting information may be provided in appendices.

Case studies

A case study is a special type of assignment and is based on a real life or fictitious business or management situation. The use of case studies as a learning and teaching activity is described in Chapter 4. You may be provided with a case study (e.g., detailed information about a particular company or situation), and asked to answer questions on it either in a written assignment or with a presentation. The type of information that you may be provided with could include: background history of the company; company accounts; sales figures; production figures; information about employees; company policies and procedures; and details about current issues facing the company or organization.

Some important points about case studies include:

- Spend time reading the case study
- Identify whether or not you will need to do additional research on the case study, e.g., do you need additional data about the organization?
- Identify whether or not you will need to do additional research, e.g., on similar companies or competitors, so that you can learn from current practice in that industry or sector?
- Identify what theoretical knowledge is relevant to the case study
- Research and read about the theoretical knowledge that is relevant to the case study
- Respond to the set questions taking care to analyse the questions and write your answers clearly
- You may be expected to make recommendations to help improve or change

the situation of the case study company. If this is the case, then make clear and explicit recommendations, ensuring that they are linked to what you have learnt from theory as well as practice.

A common problem with case studies is that students provide an imbalanced answer. For example, they use too much or too little information on the case study, relevant theoretical knowledge or their own experience. The key to doing well in case studies is to achieve a balance between your use of theoretical knowledge, the information from the case study and your own ideas. If you are uncertain as to what is expected then ask your tutor for help.

A final year student, Aimee, made the following comments about a business strategy case study:

> I enjoyed working on the case study as it brought the theory to life. We had a lot of reading to do and had to search for up-to-date company information. We discussed the case study in class and the tutor recorded the discussion. We also discussed it on Blackboard. I used this a lot when I was working on my case study assignment. For once I had too much to write and had to cut it down to fit the word count. I enjoyed case studies – we should do more – and felt it was very useful and relevant to real life.

Posters

Posters are commonly used as a means of assessing students and they involve one or a group of students producing a poster and then defending it. Typically the poster will be presented in a form of a 'gallery' with all the other students' posters and this means that they have to be visually interesting and attractive. Fundamentally, posters are used as a visual means of representing ideas and this means that too much text will often result in a low mark. They are not 'essays on walls'. Posters are commonly used in academic conferences as a means of sharing ideas.

The poster may be produced on A1 sized paper and it may be either handmade or produced using appropriate computer packages. If you are asked to produce a poster, carefully read the instructions and follow them. Preparing a poster involves:

- Working out the main messages that you want to present
- Identifying supporting evidence or examples
- Thinking about how to make your poster attractive, e.g., use of colour and images

- Identifying how you will produce the poster and relevant sources of support, e.g., colour printing, photocopying, laminating
- Producing the content of the poster
- Producing the actual poster.

When you present your poster you are likely to be asked questions about it. This means that it is important to know the content of the poster and also the origin of the ideas and evidence or examples.

Common problems with posters include:

- Lack of a clear message
- Too much or too little detail
- Large blocks of text or figures
- Lack of coherence
- Limited visual impact
- Poor physical presentation.

Presentations

Presentation skills are important as they are frequently used in the workplace as a means of both disseminating information and influencing people. Nowadays many interviews involve a formal presentation, therefore it is important to develop your presentation skills in readiness for this; the best way to developing your presentation skills is through practice.

Some of the modules on your programme of study may involve giving a presentation. This could take the form of an individual presentation or a group presentation, or you may be asked to give an informal presentation as part of a seminar. During your time as a student, it is worthwhile spending time preparing for and delivering presentations as you will find you develop useful skills for the workplace.

Preparing a presentation

Analysing the presentation

This involves answering the following questions:

- Who is the audience?
- What is the objective of the presentation?

- What is the topic?
- How long is the presentation?
- What audiovisual aids may be used to enhance to presentation, for example PowerPoint presentation, video clip (e.g., from YouTube) or Internet demonstration?

Researching the presentation

This involves identifying the main elements of the presentation title and identifying key topics or themes. Chapter 5 provides guidance on finding and evaluating relevant information.

Planning the presentation

This involves working out the order of your presentation. One frequently used presentation structure is as follows:

- Introduction: you, the topic and the presentation – its structure and organization
- The reasons why the presentation is important or relevant to the audience
- The actual topic – this may be broken down into a number of subtopics
- Implications for practice (if appropriate)
- Summary
- Ask for questions (if appropriate)
- Conclusions
- Thank the audience for listening.

Using this structure it is worthwhile identifying what is essential information and what is additional or supporting information. What *must* the audience know and what would be *nice* for them to know about the topic? This is helpful, because if you find that you are short of time then you can stick to the must know topics and if you find that you are likely to finish too early then you can develop the nice to know topics.

Making it interesting

In addition to the factual content of your presentation think about ways of making it interesting. It is common practice to provide summary or basic information using PowerPoint. You can also use this facility to present a graph, cartoon or picture containing information that is most easily presented as a visual image. In addition, short video clips (e.g., from YouTube) may be used to add interest.

Using PowerPoint

PowerPoint is a standard tool in making business presentations. However, it is often overused and it can make a presentation extremely boring. Many people talk about 'death by PowerPoint' when they sit in on presentations that use too many slides and present too much text or too many figures on each slide. Remember that presentations are face-to-face activities and that their power is in the interaction between you and your audience. Expecting your audience to read a whole list of notes on PowerPoint is both pointless and will bore them. Instead, use PowerPoint to present visual images or videoclips that help you to put across your message and make a positive impact. If you do use PowerPoint to present information a general rule is that each slide should contain no more than seven lines of information and seven words per line. If you want your audience to study some detailed information (e.g., in a table) then it is often better to present this as a handout instead.

Other forms of presentational resources include a flipchart or a whiteboard (if you wish to talk and write at the same time), handouts for your audience, a short video clip, a demonstration or even interactive role plays.

Getting organized

Break your talk into manageable chunks, each with its own heading, and jot down the main points of your talk on plain postcards or using the notes feature of PowerPoint.

Postcards look more professional than A4 paper or a notebook. They are easy to follow, as you can use one postcard for each point, flipping it to the back of the pile once you have read it. Some people staple or string them together so that if they drop them then they don't go out of order. Students sometimes lose their place during a presentation and have to spend what seems like several minutes finding the section they were up to. If you use postcards this problem is unlikely to occur as you are not looking at a great deal of information on any one sheet.

Check the facilities in the room in which you will be giving your presentation. If your PowerPoint presentation is on a disk, CD or USB memory stick then double check that the appropriate facilities are available and that you know how to use them. Remember to have a back up! It is often a good idea to email your presentation to yourself so that you can access it remotely if you have problems with the disk, etc.

Group presentations

If you are preparing for a group presentation then ensure that the team works together. If individuals go off to complete their section without any interaction with the other team members this can result in a disjointed presentation that would appear to the audience to be made of sections that don't fit together: you must work together. Prepare your PowerPoint presentation or handouts in the same style and ensure that each member uses a similar form of language. It is fine to split the research responsibilities between the group, but check each section carefully to avoid either overlaps or gaps in the information provided. It is a good idea to ask one person to edit the presentation as this helps to ensure consistency.

Decide who is going to present which section of the presentation. You may want one person doing the introduction and conclusion, with other group members presenting the different topics in the main part of the presentation. If you are working in a large group then it is possible that all group members will not be required to speak. Check this out with your tutor.

Dress appropriately if you are giving a formal presentation.

Rehearsing

It is very helpful to rehearse your presentation, so that you become comfortable with your material and your presentation aids. This also means that you can check and adjust your timing. Ask someone to watch the presentation as you rehearse and give you constructive feedback. The more time you put into preparing your presentation then the more successful it is likely to be.

If you are giving a group presentation it is particularly important to rehearse to make sure that your presentation is integrated and well organized. In particular you may find it helpful to practise the handovers from one student to another student. For example: 'I will now pass over to Ashish who is going to talk about . . .'

Giving a presentation

Before the presentation

- Prepare yourself: have a good night's sleep; eat a proper breakfast or lunch
- Arrive in plenty of time
- Organize the room: some people feel more comfortable using a lectern or table; if you are able to change the layout of the room then think about how you want the audience to sit – do you want a formal or informal seating arrangement? Do you want the chairs in theatre style, a circle or a horse shoe shape?
- Once you have organized the room sit in different seats so that you can check how different members of the audience will view your presentation
- Check how things work: light switches, electric sockets, heating, windows, blinds and computers
- Check that you have the IT elements set up and working, and run through your presentation before the audience arrives

- Check that you have the right paperwork in front of you
- Take your watch off and place it on the desk in front of you.

During the presentation

- Do not begin until your tutor and audience are settled and ready to begin listening
- If you are nervous do some deep breathing
- Let the audience know when you want to receive questions – during the presentation or at the end of it
- Help the audience to be interested in your presentation by being enthusiastic yourself
- Introduce variety by using your voice and varying the pace and tone of what you are saying
- Use your hands and facial expressions to stress certain points
- If you have practised your presentation sufficiently, you should be able to remember your main points without having to read or refer to your cards. This will give you the opportunity to talk to, rather than at, your audience, which will make you sound more interesting and will capture your audience's attention
- Maintain regular eye contact with your audience. Remember to look at the whole audience not just the tutor
- Keep an eye on the time to make sure that you are keeping to your schedule and not running out of time
- Try not to rush your presentation: pace yourself, and take a moment to catch your breath after each topic
- If you are part of a group presentation, thank the person who spoke before you and, when you have completed your section, present the next group member to the audience
- When it is time for questions, handle them with confidence: if you do not know the answer to any question be honest and say that you will find out
- When you want to close the question session signal this to your audience by saying 'We have time for one more question'
- Thank your audience when you have finished your formal presentation.

A poor presentation

Students who do poor presentations tend to:

- Be unprepared
- Be unable to use the equipment
- Start with an apology

- Read from their notes
- Make limited or no eye contact with the audience
- Focus on the tutor rather than the whole audience
- Get lost in the presentation as they don't know the material
- Rush through the presentation
- Rush off without ending the presentation properly
- Don't thank the audience.

If you are anxious about making presentations this can be dealt with in three ways. First, focus on presenting information that you know and understand. Second, you will find it easier to be enthusiastic about your presentation if you select information, ideas and examples about which you are enthusiastic. Third, rehearse your material so that you are confident about being able to present it well.

Some students use scripts as a means of tackling their nerves. However, this approach tends to backfire as they often focus all their attention on reading the script rather than engaging with the audience, who quickly become bored if there is an absence of eye contact or other forms of interaction. In contrast, if you are well prepared, have a good structure to your presentation and you are using interesting examples or images the audience is likely to be interested in your talk – even if you are sometimes searching for words and your talk is not 100 percent fluent.

A useful additional source on presentations is: Levin, P. and Topping, G. (2006) *Perfect Presentations*. Maidenhead: Open University Press.

Oral or *viva voce* examinations

Oral exams are sometime called *viva voce* exams or vivas. In this type of exam you will be questioned by one or more tutors and, in some instances, the exam may be recorded. Oral exams are used for a variety of purposes including:

- Testing a students' knowledge on a specific topic, e.g., their dissertation
- Checking that the student's exam performance reflected their knowledge and was not the result of cheating!
- Providing an opportunity for the examiner(s) to explore issues that may be difficult to express in writing – such as: challenges in gaining access to people or organizations; emotional or personal issues associated with the choice of topic; or speculative considerations of the implications of the work. In addition, some matters may be too sensitive to write about in a report but may be discussed freely in the context of the viva

- To assess the performance of students who have a borderline degree classification.

If you are involved in an oral examination then it is worthwhile preparing for it in the same way as you would for a written examination. This involves understanding the reason for the viva and what is being tested. If you are unsure then ask your tutor. You will need to revise your subject and gain practice in answering questions in an interview situation. If you are having a viva for your dissertation or thesis it is a good idea to read it carefully before you go into the viva. In addition, you may find it helpful to produce a summary on a sheet of A4 or A3 in which you identify the main themes and arguments in your work. It is a good idea to ask friends to help you prepare for and rehearse for your viva.

You will need to find out whether or not you are allowed to take notes into the viva. In some universities and colleges students are not allowed to use notes for vivas when they relate to the assessment of students who have a borderline degree mark, but they are allowed to take them in when a dissertation or thesis is being assessed. Indeed, you may be allowed to take in the dissertation or thesis as well as a set of notes.

If you have been asked to attend an oral exam because you are a borderline candidate then prepare for the exam by looking back at your exam papers or assignments and identifying any weak spots. Spend time brushing up your knowledge of these areas. It is worthwhile preparing for the oral exam by asking a friend to help you practise your answers to questions.

The structure of the oral exam is likely to be as follows:

- Introductions
- There may be some general conversation to help you settle down
- You will be told how the oral exam is going to be structured
- You will be asked a series of questions
- You may have the opportunity to give additional information to support your previous comments
- Thanks and goodbyes.

During the exam you will need to answer each question as clearly as possible. If you don't quite understand a question then do ask for clarification. If you are unsure as to whether or not you have provided sufficient detail in your answer then, again, do ask the examiners if they require more information on that topic.

If your mind goes blank ask for a couple of minutes to structure your answer. You can always give yourself time by starting off your answers with a description 'I found this topic very interesting and I particularly found the book by XXX useful; from it I learnt . . .'

Most students find that once they start talking about their subject the time quickly passes in an oral exam. At the end of the exam, remember to thank the examiners before you leave the room.

Portfolios

A portfolio is a structured collection of evidence supported by a personal statement and presented either in a folder or online. These were introduced in Chapter 3 and you may find it helpful to reread that earlier section. They are used as a means of enabling students to present themselves in a holistic manner and they are often linked with the development of employability skills or professional practice. As with all other forms of assessment, if you are asked to produce a portfolio check out the guidelines and making particular notes of the following:

- What is the purpose of the portfolio?
- What do you have to demonstrate?
- What types of evidence are you expected to include?
- Are you expected to include a personal statement that links your evidence to the learning outcomes of the assessment activity?
- How are you expected to present the portfolio – in printed or electronic format?
- What guidance are you given about how to present the portfolio?

The type of evidence that is included in a portfolio will vary depending on its purpose. One advantage of the portfolio is that it enables you to go beyond using text and you may include different visual forms such as photographs, leaflets, MindMaps or spider diagrams. In addition, you may use colour to help guide the reader through your work. This helps your portfolio to 'come alive', and it becomes engaging and interesting to read and assess.

Portfolios may include some of the following items:

- Index
- Contents page
- Introduction
- Personal statement
- *Curriculum vitae*
- Examples of your work such as: written report; examples of use of different IT packages

- Feedback on your work, e.g., from your tutor, other students, managers in the workplace
- Transcript of your assessment results
- Photographs or other images
- MindMaps or spider diagrams
- Other supporting evidence, e.g., leaflets, maps, diagrams, newspaper clippings, sample website pages
- Summary.

The following quotation provides an example from part of a student's personal statement:

Personal statement

The purpose of this portfolio is to show how I have achieved the learning outcomes of the academic and professional skills module. As a result of this module I believe I have learnt the skills required to be an effective student and I am also prepared for gaining employment.

The first section provides evidence that demonstrates how I have developed my understanding about learning and becoming a manager. I completed the learning styles questionnaire (Evidence 1) and then reflected on it (Evidence 2). This activity helped me to understand my learning strengths and weaknesses. At the end of the year, I revisited this activity and produced an updated statement (Evidence 3) and in this I show how I have become more confident and independent as a learner.

I have developed my IT skills too during the year. When I came to university I thought I had good IT skills and I scored myself highly on the self assessment quiz (Evidence 4). Once I began the IT course I realised that I had a lot to learn as I did not score highly on my diagnostic tests (Evidence 5–10). I have learnt how to use: Word; Access; Excel; EndNote and PowerPoint. I include copies of the assessed work for each of these packages (Evidence 11–15). In my reflection on this section (Evidence 16) I show that I am now more confident and can use these IT packages professionally. One advantage of these skills is that I now waste less time when I am using computers. This is a very useful set of skills both for me doing assignments and also when I come to look for a job . . .

Top quality portfolios tend to have the following characteristics:

- Very clear structure and layout
- Guide the reader, e.g., through a contents page, the index, etc.
- Highlight key information

- Use summaries
- Show that information has been carefully selected for the portfolio.

Poor quality portfolios tend to have the following characteristics:

- Too little or too much evidence
- Evidence doesn't appear to be related to the purpose of the portfolio
- Evidence lacks appropriate headings
- The reader has to work out how the evidence relates to the learning outcomes that are meant to be demonstrated in the portfolio.

If you are asked to produce a portfolio you are likely to be given a long time frame to do it in (e.g., a semester or six months). It is important that you work on your portfolio throughout this time period and that you know how it links in with the different learning and teaching activities that you are engaged in on your programme. It is likely that these are designed to help you to generate evidence for your portfolio.

> One important aspect of portfolios is that if you leave them to the last minute then you won't be able to obtain the evidence you require to complete the work.

When working on a portfolio is it always a good idea to do some work on it each week and to leave plenty of time to edit and polish it before you submit it.

Learning journals

Learning journals provide a means of developing your skills in reflection, learning more about yourself and your subject. Ideas about reflection and learning journals were first presented in Chapter 2 and they are covered in some detail in Chapter 4. If you are required to produce a learning journal as part of an assessment activity you will be given guidance on how to keep the journal and the assessment requirements.

You may be wondering, what are the characteristics of a good quality learning journal? The following list was developed by Jenny Moon (2000) and it indicates the general requirements of a good quality learning journal:

- A range of entries
- Clarity and good observation in the presentation of events or issues
- Evidence of speculation based on theory and practice
- Evidence of a willingness to revise ideas in the light of experience and discussion
- Honesty and self-assessment
- Thoroughness of reflection and self-awareness
- Depth and detail of reflective accounts
- Evidence of creative thinking
- A deep approach to the subject matter
- Representation of different cognitive skills (synthesis, analysis, evaluation, etc.)
- Evidence of reading and reference to theory
- A match of the content and outcomes of the journal work to module aim and outcomes
- Identification in the reflective process of questions for further reflection and exploration.

Plagiarism and other forms of cheating

Plagiarism

The issue of plagiarism is an important one for all students, as if you either intentionally or accidentally use the work or ideas of others without referencing them you are likely to be accused of plagiarism and the consequences are severe. This is such an important topic that this section repeats some of the key issues about plagiarism previously mentioned elsewhere in this book.

When you write your assignments, dissertation or independent study it is important that you use your own words and that you clearly identify the source of all the data, information and ideas that you use in your work. Doing this enables you to:

- Present a credible and professional piece of work
- Acknowledge the person whose work you have used in your assignment
- Make it clear which is your work and which is the work of another person
- Help the reader to track down the original sources if they want to check up or follow up interesting sources
- Demonstrate how your work links into your subject area
- Avoid accusations of stealing other people's ideas or words (plagiarism).

The basic idea is that you must state the sources of ideas and information in your assignments. This means that you must give credit to or acknowledge the original source or author whenever you:

- Use a word for word quotation from another source
- Paraphrase or use your own words to describe or summarize an idea that you have obtained from another source
- Use facts, e.g., statistical data used from another source
- Use an image or diagram from another source.

If you are unsure whether the information that you have provided should be referenced or not, then it is better to provide one to be on the safe side. The consequences of providing too many references are far less severe than those of not providing them at all or providing a list full of omissions.

If you do not acknowledge the work of others then it is seen as a form of *theft*, because you appear to be stealing other people's work and passing it off as your own work. Failure to acknowledge the sources you have used in writing your assignment is likely to result in an allegation of plagiarism being made against you. The consequences are extremely serious and range from having your mark reduced to zero to having your programme of study terminated. Some students think that if they are caught plagiarizing and their intention had not been to plagiarize, in other words that it was accidental or non-intentional, they will be excused. However, in the majority of universities and colleagues the code of practice on unfair practice or plagiarism does not distinguish between whether it was intentional or accidental plagiarism. This means that if you plagiarize a defence of, 'It was accidental', will *not* be accepted as a valid excuse.

Typically, students may be involved in one of four incidents of plagiarism:

- Plagiarism as a result of not referencing sources such as books, journal articles, websites, diagrams or images
- Plagiarism as a result of sharing work with friends
- Plagiarism through group work
- Self-plagiarism, i.e., presenting the same work in more than one assessment activity.

One of the commonest ways in which students plagiarize is by not referencing sources such as books, journal articles, websites, diagrams or images. This frequently happens when students cut and paste information from the Internet; copy paragraphs from a textbook or website, perhaps changing a few words or sentences; copy a diagram, changing a few words or the layout; or copy the work of another student. The way to avoid this form of plagiarism is to:

- Always use your own words in your assignments
- If you use the words of another person then present them as a quotation and properly reference them (see Chapter 5)
- Reference the source of *all* data, information, ideas, images, charts and diagrams used in your work (see Chapter 5).

Sometimes plagiarism arises as a result of students sharing their work with each other. This may happen quite innocently, for example friends may loan each other their draft essays and assignments, and sections are copied from one to another. Sometimes it happens because one student steals the work of a friend, for example by copying and using a file from a memory stick. However, the end result is the same – the students concerned may be accused of plagiarism and they will be treated extremely seriously through an unfair means or plagiarism procedure. If found guilty of accidental or intentional plagiarism then they may have their marks reduced to zero, they may have to resit the module or unit, and in extreme cases they may have their programme of studies terminated. Even if they are found to be innocent going through this disciplinary process is likely to be very stressful. Most business school and departments can identify students who have fallen foul of the rules of plagiarism as a result of intentional or accidental sharing of assessed work between friends. One of the sad outcomes of these situations is that it results in friends become ex-friends.

Another situation in which plagiarism may arise is in group work where one member of the group uses data, information or ideas from another source without referencing it. If this is not picked up by the group then when the work is submitted for assessment the plagiarized text is likely to be spotted by the assessor. In these situations, the whole group is normally dealt with under the unfair means or plagiarism procedure. This is because in group work the whole group takes responsibility for their work. How can you tackle this situation? It is worthwhile talking about plagiarism and correct referencing within your group and making sure that everyone understands what plagiarism is and how to avoid it. If you think that a student in your group has plagiarized the work of others then talk to them about it. If you enter the suspect text in Google, Google Scholar or in one of the plagiarism detection software packages such as Turnitin you may be able to identify the original source of the material. If you are unable to identify whether the suspect text has been copied from another source and you are still worried then it is best to go and talk to your tutor.

Finally, students sometimes self-plagiarize and this occurs when they use their work from one assignment and present it in another. In other words, they attempt to have one piece or section of work count twice towards their degree. Self-plagiarism is treated just as seriously as plagiarism from another source. It is therefore important *not* to recycle your work in different assignments.

It is important to realize that you are responsible for ensuring that the content of your academic work is properly referenced and follows standard academic practices. As explained, this relates to both individual and group work. *Plagiarism is treated very seriously by all universities*. Many universities now use specialist software, such as Turnitin, to help them to compare students' assessed work with both publicly available information (e.g., journal and websites articles), and the work of other students. Where the assessed work under scrutiny is found to be similar to another's work then it is normally investigated further and, if appropriate, the student concerned will be accused of plagiarism and taken through a disciplinary procedure. The penalties for plagiarism are normally very serious ranging from a mark of zero for the plagiarized work through to the student having their programme of study terminated. In addition, if you have been found to have plagiarized then this will be mentioned in references to a prospective employer or to another university if you want to progress to postgraduate study. Most employers would not want to employ a thief!

> If you are unsure about how to reference and acknowledge the sources that you use in your assessed work ask for help from your tutor or library.

> If you have problems with completing your assignments and handing in your work on time then talk to your tutor or the administrative support office. Do not be tempted to rush your work and not reference your sources properly. The penalties for either intentional or unintentional plagiarism are often severe and much worse than handing work in late.

Other forms of cheating

Cheating in exams is covered earlier in this chapter. Key points to remember are that all universities and colleges have good systems in place to catch cheats.

Different ways of cheating include:

- Taking prohibited materials into the exam
- Asking a friend to sit the exam for you
- Asking a friend for help during the exam
- Attempting to look at another student's answer book
- Exchanging notes in an exam
- Attempting to get hold of an unseen exam paper before the exam.

Exam invigilators spend their time looking for cheats and once they identify them they will report them to the university authorities. As with plagiarism, the consequences are likely to be serious and may result in a student being asked to leave the university.

In addition to plagiarism, students also cheat in assessed work and this may involve:

- Buying an assignment from the Internet
- Asking a family member of friend to write your assignment
- Faking the results of research.

Universities are constantly on the look out for cheats because if they get away with it their degrees are devalued. In addition, it is not fair on students who do not cheat. The penalties for cheating are high and each year students are expelled from university or college because they are caught cheating. If asked to provide a reference, the university or college will mention the expulsion and reasons for it. Employers do *not* want to employ dishonest individuals, so if you cheat this will has a long term impact on their career.

If you experience problems during your studies it is always a good idea to talk to your tutor or personal supervisor and ask them for help.

Summary

This chapter provides guidance on commonly used assessment activities including examinations, online assessment activities, assignments – essays, reports, case studies, posters, presentations, oral or *viva voce* examinations, portfolios and learning journals. It also provides advice on how to avoid accusations of plagiarism and the severe consequences of cheating. The main message in this chapter is to be prepared by making sure that you understand the assessment process and requirements. Ask your tutor for help and clarification. The theme of assessment is continued in the next chapter where the focus is on projects, dissertations and independent studies.

7

Planning and carrying out your project, dissertation or independent study

Introduction • Project management • Getting the most out of supervision sessions • Working with public, private or voluntary sector organizations • Getting started and identifying your topic • Writing your research proposal • Research approach, methodologies and methods • Writing up • Summary

Introduction

The aim of this chapter is to provide guidance to students who are carrying out an extended project, dissertation or independent study. The majority of business and management students will complete an extended piece of academic work and this work provides you with an opportunity to integrate theory and practice, demonstrate knowledge learned across a number of different modules of study, and demonstrate that you have the skills required to complete individual academic research.

The differences between projects, dissertations and independent studies will vary according to how different departments and business schools define each type of work. The following definitions provide some general guidance on the differences between these forms of work:

- A project is an assignment with a clear brief that is often work related or involves some kind of practical activity such as creating a website
- An independent study provides students with an opportunity to design their own project or research activity and to meet the assessment requirements in a flexible manner
- A dissertation is an academic research project that follows standard academic conventions.

One important differentiator between these three forms of work is the extent to which they involve a detailed academic literature review. As a generalization, dissertations involve a detailed literature review and this is in contrast to a project or independent study where the use of the research literature is less extensive. However, you are advised to find out the detailed requirements of your own department or business school.

The topics covered in this chapter include: project management, getting the most out of supervision sessions, working with public or private sector organizations, getting started and identifying your topic, writing your research proposal, identifying your research approach, research methodologies and methods, and writing up. More detailed advice is available in books such as:

- Crème, P. and Lea, M. R. (2008) *Writing at University*. Maidenhead: Open University Press.
- Levin, P. (2005) *Excellent Dissertations*. Maidenhead: Open University Press.
- Murray, N. and Hughes, G. (2008) *Writing Up Your Univeristy Assignments and Research Projects*. Maidenhead: Open University Press.

Project management

One of the reasons that students are asked to carry out project work, an independent studies or to complete a dissertation is to provide you with experience of managing your own work. You may find it helpful to use this as an opportunity to develop your project management skills and these skills are likely to be valued by your future employer. Project management typically involves the following stages.

Project analysis

- Reading and understanding the project brief and/or the assessment requirements
- If possible, look at examples of other students' work. If you look at both good quality and poor projects, independent studies or theses then this will help you to understand what is required by your tutor(s)
- Identify the general parameters of your subject (see 'getting started' below)
- Gaining approval for your proposal from your tutor
- Completing and obtaining access (if required) and ethical clearance (if required) (see later in this chapter)
- Writing up your work. At this stage it is worthwhile writing up your work, your decisions and the rationale behind them. This will mean that you keep a good record of your work.

Project plan

- Developing the project plan. You will need to identify all the tasks that you need to complete in order to finish your study. There are two main approaches to developing a plan. Table 7.1 presents a simple action plan while Figure 7.1 demonstrates a Gantt chart (named after Henry Gantt who invented it), which may be produced using a spreadsheet or specialist project management software. The action plan and Gantt chart are based on actual students' plans. If you examine them you will be able to understand why students who leave their work too late do not have sufficient time to do a good job. In particular, the final stage of writing up and editing your work often takes several months. It is this final stage of 'polishing' your work that is likely to make the difference between a mark in the 60s and one in the 70s or 80s
- Writing up your planning and development work. At this stage it is worthwhile writing up your work, your decisions and the rationale behind them. This will mean that you keep a good record of your work.

Project implementation

- Carrying out your project. This involves putting your plan into action and completing the study. While you are carrying out the study it is worthwhile checking that you are on track and that you have not drifted away from your original aims and objectives (or hypotheses)
- You may have a number of tutorials or email conversations with your tutor during this stage of your project
- Writing up your work. As you are carrying out your project it is a good idea to

Table 7.1 Simple action plan

Tasks	To be completed by
1 Produce project proposal form – 500 words	30 Oct.
2 Gain approval of project	15 Nov.
3 Complete ethics forms and gain ethics approval	15 Dec.
4 Start literature search and review	15 Oct.
5 Produce a draft literature review	15 Dec.
6 Write draft introduction and methodology	30 Jan.
7 Carry out data collection	2–30 Jan.
8 Data analysis	1–28 Feb.
9 Write draft findings	5 Mar.
10 Edit and update literature review	5 Mar.
11 Write discussion and conclusions	30 Mar.
12 Edit whole work	1–31 Apr.
13 Bind and prepare for presentation	1–5 May
14 Hand in work	7 May

write up your work. This is normally time consuming and involves drafting and redrafting your work (see later in this chapter)
- Completing the project. This involves completing all the assessment requirements and handing in your work.

Project evaluation and review

- Evaluating and reviewing the project process and outcomes. This involves weighing up your project process and reflecting on it. Sometimes this reflection process is included in the assessment requirements and you will need to include it in your project, independent study or dissertation. Even if you are not required to produce a reflective statement for your assessed work it is still well worth carrying this out as it will enable you to learn from the process of completing an extended piece of work.

Getting the most out of supervision sessions

If you are carrying out an extended project, dissertation or independent study then you will normally be allocated a supervisor who will support you in your work. Universities and colleges organize the supervision of student projects in different ways so it is important to find out how the supervision system is

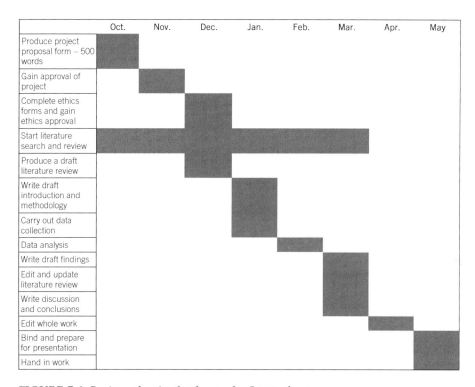

	Oct.	Nov.	Dec.	Jan.	Feb.	Mar.	Apr.	May
Produce project proposal form – 500 words	■							
Gain approval of project		■						
Complete ethics forms and gain ethics approval			■					
Start literature search and review	■	■	■	■	■	■		
Produce a draft literature review			■					
Write draft introduction and methodology				■				
Carry out data collection				■				
Data analysis					■			
Write draft findings						■		
Edit and update literature review						■		
Write discussion and conclusions						■		
Edit whole work							■	
Bind and prepare for presentation								■
Hand in work								■

FIGURE 7.1 Project plan in the form of a Gantt chart

organized, and the type and frequency of contact you may expect to have with your supervisor.

There are three main methods of supervision:

- Group supervision. Some departments organize students into small groups who are then supervised by one supervisor. One of the advantages of this approach is that in the supervision sessions you will learn from the issues and questions raised by other students.
- Individual supervision. This is the traditional method of supervision where you have the opportunity for one to one supervision
- Mixed supervision. In this approach, supervision starts off with small group supervision sessions and then moves to one to one supervision sessions when students are writing up their work.

Your supervisor's role is to be supportive, give you academic advice and to be constructively critical. You will be able to contact your supervisor by email or in person. Supervision sessions provide you with a valuable opportunity to gain individual help and also to have your queries or problems dealt with by your supervisor. The following list of tips will help you to get the most out of these sessions:

- Make an arrangement to see your supervisor as early as possible in the life of your project, dissertation or independent study
- Be on time
- Be prepared by coming along with a list of questions
- If you are asked to prepare for the tutorial then make sure you have carried out this work in advance of your tutorial
- Keep your tutor informed of your progress
- If you are going on holiday, inform your tutor.

It is worthwhile remembering that although your project, dissertation or independent study may be the main focus of your studies and life, it is likely to be routine and part of the academic cycle for your tutor or supervisor. They will be involved in other activities too, such as teaching, assessment and research. In addition, they may be scheduled to take holidays during your work on the project, dissertation or independent study. This means that it is important that you plan ahead and discuss with them how you will work together, identifying holiday periods when your supervisor will not be available. This will help to ensure that your work on your project, dissertation or independent study runs smoothly.

When you come to write up your work it is important to find out what level of support you can expect from your supervisor. Different departments and business schools have their own rules about how much support is available. For example, some will encourage supervisors to read and give feedback on draft chapters while in other institutions this is forbidden.

Working with public, private or voluntary sector organizations

Many students carry out a workplace project or research for a company, public sector or voluntary organization. This has a number of benefits:

- You obtain some 'real life' experience
- You will be able to link theory and practice

- You will be able to carry out a project or research that will inform the organization's practices
- The organization will gain from your knowledge and expertise
- You will get to know one organization well and they will get to know you
- You will extend your business networks.

However, there are some risks related to carrying out workplace projects or research, and these include:

- Difficulty in obtaining access and permission to carry out the work
- Difficulty in making appointments with key people due to the pressures of their work
- Key people leaving the organization meaning that you no longer have access to them, certain resources or facilities
- Change in workload pressures on the organization meaning that they no longer have time for you and your project
- Producing results that are uncomfortable or challenging for the organization
- A manager or director changes their mind about you carrying out your work after you have already invested a lot of time and energy into the project or research.

Your department or business school may employ staff whose role it is to help their students work with businesses and other organizations. Similarly, some companies will ask one of their employees to act as a mentor to the student. There are ways in which you can help ensure that your workplace project or research is successful and common strategies for managing workplace projects and research include:

- Presenting the company or organization with a written project or research proposal that makes it very clear what is involved in the piece of work in terms of who, what, when, where, how
- Discussing and clarifying the expectations of the organization as well as your expectations in terms of carrying out an academic workplace project or piece of research
- Discussing issues of confidentiality, data protection and intellectual property. Agreeing how these will be managed within the project or research
- Gaining written permission for the project or research from senior managers
- Agreeing how to communicate the project or research process to the company or organization.

If you are carrying out a workplace project or piece of research it is worth spending time at the start of the process in establishing how you will work with your organization. Your business school or department will provide you with help and advice, and if major problems arise then it is important to contact your supervisor as soon as possible. Remember there are major benefits to carrying out workplace projects and research, and many students find that it can lead to employment opportunities in the future.

Getting started and identifying your topic

Some textbooks on carrying out projects, research or independent studies give the impression that the process is linear with a clear beginning, middle and end. In reality, the process is often iterative as the student develops their ideas and amends their research or project in the light of their reading about research, their literature review or their fieldwork.

The best starting point is to identify a topic that you find interesting and one that you want to explore in detail. Some projects or dissertations may take place over the course of a whole academic year and so it is important to choose something that you find interesting and that you feel motivated towards working on.

Activity 7.1 Getting started

The aim of this activity is to help you to start working on your project, independent study or dissertation, and to start identifying the main theme and topics. Completing Table 7.2 will provide you with a starting point and something that you can discuss with your tutor or supervisor. Once you have identified some key aspects of the topic that you wish to explore you will need to identify your topic in much more depth.

In the majority of academic studies you will be required to link your research to the existing literature. Consequently, it is a good idea to carry out a literature search (see Chapter 5) as soon as possible. This will help you identify whether or not there is a literature base in this area and also the key authors and researchers in the field. Further, the literature review is likely to provide you with ideas about your research approach, methodology and methods as well as some of the problems other researchers have encountered in this area of study. Many students find that they need to return to and change their research aim and hypotheses or questions as a result of their literature review. This is a normal part of the research process and it indicates that your study is likely to be in line with established research in the field.

Table 7.2 Getting started on your project or research

Working title

Proposed aim of the project, independent study or dissertation

Draft research questions or project aim and outcomes

Keywords or topics

Relevant information sources

Proposed methodology

Ethical issues

Notes

Writing your research proposal

Once you have gained approval for your idea then you are likely to be asked to produce a proposal. This is a document that outlines what you intend to do in your workplace project, dissertation or independent study. Typically proposals may be between 500 and 2000 words long. Many modules or courses include a section on writing a proposal as part of the assessment process. If this applies to you then be careful to read the assessment criteria before starting your proposal.

Typical headings for organizing a proposal are likely to include:

- Title
- Introduction, containing:
  - project aims and objectives or research aims and hypotheses/questions
  - problem or issue to be addressed
  - context of the work, e.g., specific company or sector

  - scope of the work, e.g., what is going to be included and what is going to be excluded
- Relevant literature. This will indicate the literature base for the work and key items (e.g., books or journal articles). It may also include an outline literature and information search strategy, e.g., which business databases you will search for up to date information on the topic. This topic was covered in Chapter 5. You may use this section to justify your proposed research methods and to highlight potential problems that other researchers have experienced in this field. In some workplace projects or independent studies this section may be extremely small
- Context of the study. This section will provide a summary of the organization or business, or the business sector, e.g., health care products, logistics and supply chain management. Desk based research not linked to a particular organization will not necessarily include this section.
- Proposed methodology:
  - In dissertations, this section will present your research approach, methodology and methods including data collection and data analysis methods. It will also consider issues of access and ethics. It is likely that this section will be informed by your literature research and that your proposed methodology is in alignment with what is commonly used in your field of study. These topics are covered in the next section
  - In workplace projects or independent studies, this section may take a different form, relevant to the particular project or study
- Action plan. This will provide a detailed time schedule for your work. See Table 7.1 and Figure 7.1
- Resource requirements, e.g., any special resources that you will need in order to carry out your work
- Initial list of references.

One common question asked by students about writing proposals is: 'How much detail should I put into my proposal?' Ask your tutor for guidance. However, the more detail you put into your proposal the easier it will be to assess whether or not your work is feasible within the given constraints.

Research approach, methodologies and methods

There is a vast literature on research and research methodologies for business and management students. The purpose of this section is to provide a general overview of the approaches taken by many students. You are advised to refer to additional research methods textbooks before starting your own work. Useful starting points include:

- Bryman, A. and Bell, E. (2006) *Business Research Methods*, 2nd edn. Oxford: Oxford University Press.
- Robson, C. (2002) *Real World Research*. Oxford: Blackwell.
- Saunders, M., Thornhill, A. and Lewis, P. (2006) *Research Methods for Business Students*, 4th edn. London: Prentice Hall.

The following diagram (Figure 7.2) provides an overview of the concepts that you will need to think about as you decide on your research approach, methodology and methods. This is sometimes called the research onion (source unknown) and you need to start on the outside, working into the centre. This process is replicated in this section and Figure 7.3 (later in the chapter) provides a detailed diagram of this process.

Research approach

There are a number of different research approaches and two main approaches are the subjectivist, sometimes called the interpretivist approach, and the objectivist or the positivist approach. Your research approach depends on your view of the world. The selection of your research approach involves considering three sets of assumptions: ontological, epistemological, and assumptions concerning human nature and agency. These approaches are outlined in Table 7.3.

Ontology is concerned with the nature of the social phenomena being studied and it is typified through two positions: nominalist or realist. The nominalist position views the world as something that is socially constructed and researching this world involves collecting subjective accounts and experiences (i.e., qualitative data). In contrast the realist position sees the world as given and separate from individuals; it can be researched through 'objective' data and involves using positivist, scientific and experimental methodologies involving quantitative data. This dichotomy of nominalist and realist positions is an oversimplification as even traditionally realist approaches, such as in scientific research, are socially constructed (Bryman and Bell 2007).

The second set of assumptions is concerned with epistemology or the nature of knowledge. The positivist view is that knowledge is hard, objective and quantifiable, and research from this perspective involves 'objective' observers collecting and analysing quantitative data. The antipositivist view is that knowledge is softer, subjective and based on individual experience and, as a result, the 'subjective' researcher must be taken into account during the development and implementation of a research project as their involvement in the research project will have an impact on the research process and outcomes.

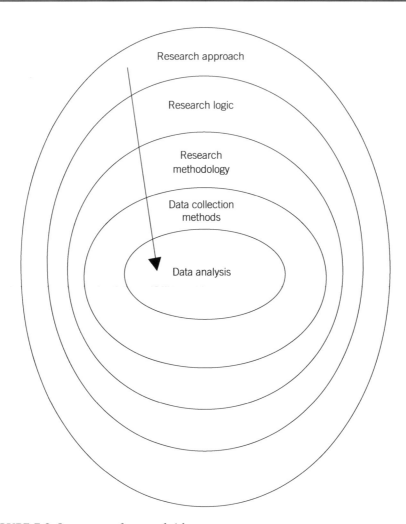

FIGURE 7.2 Summary of research ideas

The third set of assumptions is concerned with human nature and agency, in other words the perspective that individuals act voluntarily (voluntarism) or the perspective that their behaviour is predetermined (determinism), for example by instinct. Researchers who believe in the latter are likely to select scientific approaches to research involving experiments and measuring observations while people who believe in voluntarism are likely to use research methodologies and methods that will enable them to explain and understand their world.

Table 7.3 Overview of research approaches

Subjectivist approach to social science		The objectivist approach to social science
Nominalism	**Ontology**	Realism
Antipositivism	**Epistemology**	Positivism
Voluntarism	**Human Nature**	Determinism

Many students find that it takes some time to get to grips with these theoretical ideas about research. However, it is important to understand them as this will help you to produce a high quality dissertation and it also informs many workplace projects or independent studies. How do you decide on your research approach? A simple way forward is to make your decision on the basis of:

- Your own preferences, e.g., do you want to carry out quantitative or qualitative research? If you want to carry out qualitative research then you will be taking a subjectivist approach and if you want to carry out quantitative research then you will be taking an objectivist approach (see Table 7.3)
- The dominant approach to research in your chosen field of interest. Using the same methodological approach as that which is commonly used by other researchers in your specific field of interest will help you to link your ideas and findings with those in the current research literature
- The dominant approach in the organization or context of our study. For example, many practitioners in the health service work with a scientific or positivist perspective. This may mean that they are more likely to find a project or research based on this perspective more compelling than a subjectivist or interpretivist piece of work
- Advice and guidance from your tutor or supervisor.

If you decide to take a subjectivist approach and carry out qualitative work then it is likely that your study will involve inductive reasoning. This means that your work will involve:

- Identifying your research aim
- Identifying research questions
- Identifying your methodological approach
- Data collection
- Data analysis resulting in the identification of patterns or trends
- Development of tentative conclusions.

If you decide to take an objectivist approach and carry out quantitative work then it is likely that your study will involve deductive reasoning. This means that your work will involve:

- Identifying your research aim
- Identifying research hypotheses
- Identifying your methodological approach
- Data collection
- Data analysis resulting in testing your hypotheses
- Development of tentative conclusions

Methodological approach

The term 'methodology' refers to the theory of acquiring new knowledge and the processes involved in identifying, reflecting upon and justifying the best research methods. Research methodology is the process of identifying, selecting and justifying the methods used to collect the data that will provide the evidence base for generating or confirming knowledge. The research methodology involves considering the overall theoretical approach to the study and ensuring that the methodology is in alignment with the research aims and questions (or hypotheses), the theoretical framework of the study and the underpinning literature base. If the research is in alignment with the specific field of knowledge in which it is located then any knowledge generated is likely to be accepted by other researchers within this field and so will contribute to the development of the knowledge base.

The next step in the research is to identify the methodological approach. There are many different methodological approaches used in projects and studies in the fields of business and management. This are listed in Table 7.4 which also categorizes them according to whether or not they are commonly used in subjectivist or objectivist studies. Some methods may be used in both types of research (e.g., surveys). Further information about each of these different approaches is available in standard research methods books.

Table 7.4 Different methodological approaches

Subjectivist approaches	Objectivist approaches
Action research	Correlation research
Case studies	Historical research
Ethnographic research	Scientific experiment
Historical research	Surveys
Surveys	

Once you have selected your methodological approach then it is worthwhile reading up about them and getting to grips with their advantages and disadvantages. Read up to date journal articles in your field of interest and study the methodological approaches used by current researchers. This will help to inform your study and it will help ground it in current research practice rather than the more theoretical descriptions provided by research methods textbooks.

Data collection

Commonly used data collection methods include: questionnaires, interviews, focus groups, data available via computer systems, research diaries and learning journals. You will need to think through your research process and design your detailed data collection methods to make sure that the data collection method you use enables you to fulfil the aims of your study and your research questions or hypotheses. A common error made in some student research projects is that the students quickly design questionnaires or interview schedules without thinking about how they are going to analyse their data and whether or not it will provide them with the information they require to meet the aims of their project. By the time they realize that their research process has gone astray – as a result of a badly designed questionnaire – it is too late to remedy the situation.

Data collection often appears to be deceptively simple when you are sitting in a lecture or tutorial. However, if this stage goes wrong your whole project will be at risk. It is safest to assume that the data are *not* available until you have actually obtained them. Each year there are some business and management students who, after months of working on their questionnaires or interviews, find that their research participants are not available or that the permission they were given to question employees in an organization has suddenly been withdrawn due to pressures of work or the appointment of a new manager. This problem regularly arises with workplace projects and research where your work as a student researcher is very low on the real life priorities of the organization; if the organization is facing any difficulties it is likely to focus on its core business rather than support a student's project. Consequently, it is sensible to have a contingency plan so that your work is not a write-off if you are unable to obtain the required data.

Qualitative data analysis

If you are carrying out a research project or independent study using qualitative data then the data analysis process is likely to involve identifying general patterns or themes in your data. A helpful starting point is to skim through and become familiar with the data and start identifying general themes.

Many researchers use coding systems to classify the data into categories and make sense of their data. There are two distinct approaches to content analysis: *de novo* analysis in which codes are developed from the data itself and the use of a predetermined coding scheme.

Many qualitative researchers use software packages to help organize and analyse their data and a commonly used example is NVivo. If you are using this type of package then you will need to convert your data from questionnaires or interviews into an electronic format such as a Word document before uploading them into NVivo. You will then be able to organize and manipulate your data using general keywords or themes.

The next stage in the research process involved what Radnor (2001) calls 'analysis to interpretation' and it is concerned with interpreting the findings and developing meaning from them. The first stage of this involves writing statements that summarize the data organized into categories (as outlined above). These are then worked with and used to develop an explanation of the findings.

Quantitative data analysis

The most common approach to quantitative data analysis is through the use of statistical methods and through the use of computer packages such as SPSS. If you use a package such as SPSS then you will need to input your data into the package and then you will be able to manipulate it using standard statistical measures. Once you have obtained the results from this analysis then you will need to interpret them and relate your findings to your original hypotheses.

Access and ethical issues

An important issue in all research studies and projects is that of obtaining access for the study. If you wish to carry out a study in an organization where you are employed you will need to obtain the written consent of the appropriate managers or directors. In some organizations, such as the NHS, you will also need to apply for ethical clearance to carry out your research. This process may take a long time so you need to build it into your action plan.

Your business school or department will require you to obtain ethical clearance to carry out your research study or project. This normally means filling out a standard set of forms in which you outline what you intend to do and also how you will be carrying out research to the required ethical standards. Before you complete these forms, you need to consider ethical issues and work out how you will ensure that your research meets the required ethical standards. Common issues include: data storage and ensuring the maintenance of participants' confidentiality and anonymity; and how to obtain informed consent. When considering the data that you collect in your study you will need to reflect on whether or not you will be able to keep it secure, for example in a locked cabinet or accessible only via passwords on a computer. You will also need to think about how you separate data identifying individuals from your questionnaires, interviews or focus groups. Another issue is that of seeking informed consent and there is a danger that this is treated as simply a procedure of asking participants to complete and sign an informed consent form. Rather, you must ensure that your participants have a good understanding of what they are agreeing to and that they can withdraw from the research at any time. Many researchers provide a draft copy of their work to the participants who then have the opportunity to suggest changes or amendments to the information that they have provided before producing a final version. If you are intending to carry out an experiment or work with children or vulnerable adults then you may have to gain special permission. As part of the ethics procedure, you will also need to demonstrate that you will maintain anonymity and confidentiality of the people involved in your research.

In addition, you will need to consider how you work with any participating organizations on your research or project. You will find it useful to talk to them about a range of issues such as what they can expect from you in terms of your working practices, confidentiality, informed consent, intellectual property, etc. Important issues that need to be resolved include: do you maintain the organization's anonymity in your work? Who has access to your work? Do you provide the host organization with the same work that you hand in to your department or business school or do they require a separate version? You will also need to talk to them about your final output (i.e., the project, theses or independent study). Some organizations have concerns over confidentiality and who will have access to your study, and you may find it helpful to explain the assessment process. This may involve explaining that in the UK assignments are normally marked by a tutor and then either second marked or moderated by another tutor, and finally they may then be viewed by an external examiner. The work is normally kept under lock and key during this process though it may be sent by recorded mail to an examiner. Some organizations request that the work is marked confidential and that access to it is strictly limited at all times. Some organizations will state that your research or project may not be published in whole or in part in any public publication (including websites). In addition, some business schools or departments maintain a library copy of all projects and dissertations, and some organizations that permit students to carry out research on them may require that the work is not available through open access. Finally, the organization may ask you to sign a nondisclosure agreement in which you promise to keep the findings of your work confidential and not disclose them to their competitors or any future employer.

Many business schools and universities provide specialist advice to students on carrying out research or projects with external organizations.

You will normally be introduced to the ethical practices and procedures in your department or business school either as part of a research methods module or as part of your project, independent study or dissertation module. If you have any concerns about this aspect of your work then it is important to ask your tutor for help.

Summarizing the research process

One method of summarizing the research approach and methodology is using what is sometimes called 'the research onion' (source unknown) and this was first presented in Figure 7.2. Figure 7.3 shows the different levels of thought and activity that take place during a research or work based project. When you are writing up your research proposal and thinking about your research approach and methods then it is best to start on the outside layer of the diagram with either a subjectivist/interpretivist approach or objectivist/positivist approach and then work through to the centre of the diagram. Using this approach will help you to ensure your work is logical and consistent. However, it is worthwhile remembering that this is a simplification of the research process and you are advised to read research methods textbooks to develop your knowledge of this topic.

Reminder: if you are carrying out a workplace project or independent study then you may not be required to provide this level of detail or theory in your work. You will need to check with your tutor or supervisor to find out their expectations in terms of writing up your methodology.

Research issues

In all research studies or projects there is a need to ensure that your work is of good quality. In traditional research projects there are some standards approaches used to determine good quality research, and different measures are used for both qualitative and quantitative projects.

If you carry out a qualitative study then you need to consider issues of credibility, transferability, dependability and conformability (Bryman and Bell 2007).

* *Credibility*. Credibility relates to producing a credible account of the subject of your research and this involves producing an accurate account and one that is not made up, selective or distorted. Another aspect of producing a credible account relates to whether or not the study fairly represents the perspectives of different people and stakeholders relevant to the study

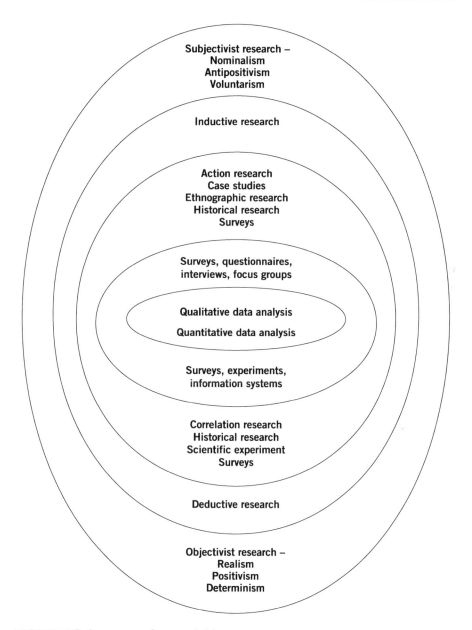

FIGURE 7.3 Summary of research ideas

- *Transferability*. Transferability relates to the possibility of transferring the findings from the particular qualitative study to other situations
- *Dependability*. Dependability involves validating findings and ensuring that there is an audit trail. The use of a range of different data sources will help to produce dependable findings and hence to build up an accurate picture of the focus of the study
- *Confirmability*. Confirmability relates to the idea that as a researcher you take appropriate steps to ensure that you don't affect the research outcomes, e.g., as a result of your beliefs or interests.

If you carry out a quantitative study then you need to consider issues of validity, reliability and generalizability (Bryman and Bell 2007).

- *Validity*. Validity is concerned with ensuring that the research is 'accurate' or 'truthful', e.g., have you measured what they said they would measure? Have you used appropriate methods to select your sample? Is the sample of an appropriate size? What sources of bias might exist in the study? How have these been addressed?
- *Reliability*. Reliability is concerned with consistency and replicability. If another researcher carried out the same study with the same methods in a similar context would they produce the same results as those you produced?
- *Generalizability*. This concept relates to the idea that the findings from positivist research can be generalized to other situations or contexts.

One technique for ensuring that quantitative research is valid and reliable is through 'triangulation' and this involves using multiple data sources as a means of creating an accurate account of the research (Bryman and Bell 2007).

This section provides a simple overview of the different concepts used in the research process. In reality, the research process is much more complicated than this and you are advised to use specialist textbooks on research methods in business and management to help you design and write up your research process.

> *Reminder*: if you are carrying out a workplace project or independent study then you may not be required to provide this level of detail or theory in your work. You will need to check with your tutor or supervisor to find out their expectations in terms of writing up your work.

Writing up

As suggested earlier in this chapter, the writing up process is best started early in the life of the project or research. If you write up as you carry out your work then you are likely to find that you capture important details at the time that they are happening. In addition, it helps to reduce the amount of writing that you will need to do at the end of your study.

One decision that you need to make about writing up your work relates to the style and structure of your work. You need to think about the reader, who may be a lecturer assessing your work or a manager in the workplace. Check out the required style by talking to your supervisor and also by reading the relevant guidance materials. You will need to work out a structure or set of headings for your work and you may find that your proposal provides a good starting point. Below are three example structures.

Workplace project structure: an example

- Title page
- Executive summary
- Introduction
- Context of the study
- Current practices
- Methodology
- Findings
- Evaluation of findings
- Implications for practice
- Recommendations
- Conclusions
- List of references.

Independent study report structure: an example

- Summary report
  - Title page
  - Abstract
  - Introduction
  - Methodology
  - The product
  - Critical evaluation
  - Summary
  - List of references

- Product:
  - Training DVD
  - Printed supporting materials for trainer and trainee
- Reflective summary
  - Personal statement.

Dissertation structure: an example

- Title page
- Abstract
- Introduction
- Literature review
- Methodology
- Findings
- Discussions
- Critique of the study
- Conclusions
- List of references
- Appendices.

It is normal practice to use headings and subheadings as a means of guiding the reader, and one commonly used format is:

- Level 1 **CHAPTER HEADINGS** (upper case, bold)
- Level 2 **Subheadings** (lower case, bold)
- Level 3 *Sub-subheadings* (lower case, italics).

If you use more than three levels then it can become confusing for the reader. Keep to a simple structure and use it consistently; this will help guide the reader through your work. Within each section or subsection you may find it helpful to structure your work in the following way:

- Introduction to the section
- Topic 1
- Topic 2
- Topic 3
- Conclusion or summary of section.

Alternatively, you could structure it as follows:

- Introduction to the section
- Advantages: topic 1, topic 2, topic 3

- Disadvantages: topic 1, topic 2, topic 3
- Conclusion or summary of section.

It is worthwhile spending some time working out how to structure your ideas. Techniques that may help you to structure your work include:

- Writing down each of the topics or themes on a Post-it note and then organizing them into a logical order
- Imagine that you have been asked to produce a presentation on your work and produce a PowerPoint presentation that will enable you to cover all the topics that you will include in your write-up
- Use MindMapping or a spider diagram to sort out and structure your ideas.

Wellington *et al.* (2005) provide a helpful guide to structuring your work and this involves using four strategies within the text. These are:

- *Signposting*, i.e., letting the reader know the structure of the work. Examples include: 'This chapter describes . . .' or 'This section outlines three main themes'
- *Framing*, i.e., marking the beginning and endings of chapters or sections. Examples include the use of phrases such as: 'First . . .', 'Finally . . .' or 'To conclude . . .'
- *Linking*, i.e., providing connections between sentences, sections or chapters. Examples include: 'In the next section . . .' or 'This topic is explored in more detail in the next chapter . . .'
- *Focusing*, i.e., highlighting or emphasizing important points. Examples include: 'The main point . . .' or 'An important point mentioned in the previous chapter . . .'

Getting started with writing

The best way to write up your work is to start with a section or topic that you feel confident about and then start writing. Focus on writing down the main ideas and don't expect to produce a perfect draft first time.

If you have difficulties getting started then imagine that you are describing your work to a friend or tutor and write down your words. One tip is never to stop writing when you reach the end of a section but instead start the next section and then stop. This means that when you next start writing you already have some words to work from.

Here are some common strategies for getting started with writing:

- Plan out your work on a large sheet of paper

- Make a list of headings and start to write key ideas or themes under each heading
- Talk to a friend about your work
- Talk out loud or into a digital recorder
- Start writing and see what happens
- Start writing and ignore any errors. You can always come back and edit your work
- Set yourself a target of at least 200 words per day and write until you have completed your target.

Once you have got a basic draft of your work you will need to edit it and individual students will edit their work in different ways. Here are five ways of editing and improving your work:

1 Checking for the accuracy and relevance of content and the logical ordering of ideas
2 Reading and improving the flow of words
3 Introducing an internal structure using signposting, framing, linking and focusing (see above)
4 Checking referencing
5 Checking for correct spelling, punctuation and grammar.

This process is probably best carried out as five separate activities and some people prefer to edit from the computer screen while others prefer to print out their work. This editing process takes a long time and it is often best to leave your work on one side for a few days and then return to it and edit it again. It is worthwhile asking family or friends to check your work for you too. Even if they don't know about the subject they will be able to give you helpful feedback as to whether or not your writing is clear and logical, and whether there are any spelling or grammatical errors.

Tips for writing up:

1 Start writing as early as possible
2 Decide on your style and tone
    - Use of the first or third person (I or one)
    - Use of active or passive verbs (active – 'I wrote the report'; or passive – 'The report was written')
3 There is no perfect time to write; it is best to start writing as soon as possible
4 People who read a lot often find it easier to write. The more you read about your subject then the more you will understand it and its language. Use a favourite textbook as a model for your own writing. However, *beware of plagiarism*

5 Talk about your subject and work. The more you talk about your work, e.g., in supervision sessions or with your friends, the easier you will find it to write up

6 if you find it hard to write then imagine you are explaining your work to a friend or tutor

7 Divide your written work into sections and subsections using headings and subheadings

8 Some people find it easiest to start with their favourite topic, while others like to start at the beginning and work through to the end

9 Do not expect to get it right first time. You will need to produce a number of drafts and edit your work many times before you get it right

10 Be honest in your write up. Explain what worked or what didn't work in your project or research. Identify and attempt to clarify contradictions or the messiness that often appears in real life research and projects

11 Introduce an internal structure using signposting, framing, linking and focusing

12 Do not use very long sentences and make sure that each paragraph contains at least three sentences. Vary the length of sentences as this helps to give your work variety

13 Avoid using clichés such as, 'It is a well known fact . . .' or 'On a level playing field'

14 Read and edit your work at least three times

15 Ask a friend to read and comment on your work

16 Remember to keep checking the assessment criteria and to follow them in great detail.

Finally, if your basic English skills such as spelling, grammar or punctuation are weak then it is worthwhile investing time and energy in improving them. Most universities and colleges provide study and language support in these areas.

Summary

This chapter provides guidance to students who are carrying out an extended project, dissertation or independent study. The topics covered in this chapter include: project management, getting the most out of supervision sessions, working with public or private sector organizations, getting started and identifying your topic, writing your research proposal, identifying your research approach, research methodologies and methods, and writing up.

Although the topics presented in this chapter are presented in a linear form, in reality most students work through an iterative process. For example, you may find that you change your proposed methodology in response to findings from the literature review or the challenges of carrying out a live project or research. In addition, writing up is not a process that starts at the end of the project or research. Instead, it is best started early and developed as you complete your work.

8

Working in groups

Introduction • Reasons for using group work • Effective student groups
• Organizing and getting the most out of meetings • Working in diverse groups
• Virtual groups • Common problems in group work • Managing the emotional
aspects of group work • Summary

Introduction

The aim of this chapter is to provide you with guidance on working in groups and, in particular, on assessed group work. The topics covered in this chapter include:

- Reasons for using group work
- Effective student groups
- Organizing and getting the most out of meetings
- Working in diverse groups
- Virtual groups
- Common problems in group work
- Managing the emotional aspects of group work.

The ability to work in teams and, in particular, diverse or international teams is an essential skill for anyone who wants to work in an organization. Most employers value highly individuals with excellent group or team working skills and they seek them out during their recruitment processes. Actively engaging in group work during your degree programme will help you to improve your skills and it will also give you good examples to use in interviews.

A useful additional resource on this topic is: Levin, P. (2004) *Successful Teamwork!* Buckingham: Open University Press.

Reasons for using group work

During your programme of study you will be asked to work in groups and some of your assessment activities will involve group work, e.g. a group presentation or a group project. Business and management students typically experience different types of group work such as:

- Activity groups where three or four students work on a specific activity as part of a tutorial or seminar
- Assessment groups where the group produces some kind of group product that will be assessed
- Online groups where the group meet and work together in a virtual environment
- Study groups where a small group of students meet together to study a particular topic or subject
- Revision groups where a small group of students meet together to revise for an examination.

This list of examples suggests that there are two main types of groups: those set up by a tutor, for example as part of a seminar or tutorial activity, and those that are self-managed, for example study or revision groups.

One of the reasons for including opportunities for group work in your programme of study relates to social theories of learning (see Chapter 3). These suggest that working in groups provides opportunities to:

- Share ideas and experiences
- Develop an understanding of different perspectives, e.g., if you work in a group with students from all around the world then you will gain an international perspective
- Stimulate ideas and creativity
- Gain experience in talking about your subject. This tends to help promote writing skills too
- Share a task that may be too large for one person
- Provide variety to the module or course
- Make friends
- Learn to lead or be part of a group.

The last reason (Learn to lead or be part of a group) is a common rationale behind group work on business or management programmes. Group work provides opportunities for you to develop and demonstrate transferable skills that are required by employers such as communication skills, negotiation skills, decision making skills, and, obviously, group work skills. In addition, the academic content of some business and management modules (e.g., managing people, management and organizational behaviour) is concerned with theories of group work and the process of working in a group provides opportunities to link your practical experiences with the theory. This chapter will help you to identify different ways of approaching group work so that it becomes a successful and (hopefully) enjoyable experience.

Effective student groups

Here are some comments from students about their experiences of assessed group work:

> It was very easy. We got well organised and agreed to meet every fortnight. We spent some time getting to know each other. We shared the work out and everyone kept their promises and delivered on time. If we couldn't attend a meeting then we texted each other. By the end of the assignment we were all good friends and we got a high mark.

> It was hard arranging a time to meet up. After a month of hassle and wasted time we decided to meet every Monday after the main lecture. This worked well and after that we got on with the assignment. We got a good mark.

> Our group never got going. We never all met up and the presentation was poor. It was obvious that we hadn't planned it – there was a lot of repetition and it was a bit boring. We got a poor mark and we deserved it.

> The group work was hard. All the other group members lived in hall and they began to meet up in hall and make decisions without me. I felt left out. In the end I spoke to the tutor and she raised it as an issue in the tutorial. The other students were

upset as they hadn't realised I felt left out and they would have preferred me to talk to them direct. After that we met on campus during the day and the group worked well together.

We only met up twice but we kept in contact by Blackboard. It worked well (to my surprise). I found I had to go onto Blackboard every day which was a pain.

Effective student group work often shows the following characteristics.

- Well organized – students arrange to meet at the same time/place on a regular basis, everyone attends, they keep a record of their activities and agreed actions, monitoring their progress against the deadline
- Manage the process – students spend time getting to know each other, they support each other and include everyone
- Communication – students listen to each other, they give everyone a chance to join in, they keep in regular touch with each other.

Table 8.1 provides a list of helpful behaviours in group work and gives examples of each behaviour.

Activity 8.1 Developing your group work skills

The aim of this activity is to help you to identify behaviours that are helpful in group work. Table 8.2 provides an inventory of helpful behaviours in group work. The next time you are involved in group work identify which of the behaviours you demonstrate by placing a tick in the relevant row each time you demonstrate the behaviour. Once you have completed the group meeting or activity then reflect on the table. Identify the rows with the smallest number of ticks and practise these behaviours at the next appropriate opportunity. This will help you to improve your group work skills.

You may find it helpful to ask everyone in the group to complete this exercise and this will help you all to improve your skills. It will also help to make the group work process more productive.

Table 8.1 Helpful behaviours in group work

Behaviour	Examples
Supporting each other	Example phrase: 'That's helpful'
Listening to other students by giving them your full attention	Use your body language, e.g., good eye contact and supportive nods, to indicate that you are listening
Encouraging each other	Example phrase: 'I am sure you can do it'
Helping the flow	Examples include contributing to discussions, asking questions, encouraging everyone to take part, signaling the beginning and end of meetings. It can also involve providing summaries and helping everyone to keep in touch between meetings.
Making suggestions	Example phrase: 'What about . . .'
Giving praise	Example phrase: 'Well done' or 'I like that diagram'
Being honest	Example phrase: 'I feel uncomfortable saying this . . .'
Admitting mistakes	Example phrase: 'I'm sorry but I didn't manage to . . .'
Sharing information and ideas	Example phrase: 'I found some useful information at this website'
Working cooperatively	Example phrase: 'I'll do the introduction if someone else will write up the methodology'
Being prepared to compromise	Example phrase: 'What about compromising and using John's outline and Jane's diagrams'
Giving constructive criticism	Example phrase: 'I may be misunderstanding what we agreed but I thought Bushra was going to . . .'
Dealing with disagreements constructively by clarifying your understanding	Example phrase: 'Have you thought about . . .' or 'I wonder what would happen if . . .'
Providing summaries	Example phrase: 'Well it looks as if we have agreed to . . .'
Keeping promises	Examples include keeping to deadlines and producing any promised work

Organizing and getting the most out of meetings

The first step in group work is to meet up! The start of group work is often signaled by a tutor either providing a list of groups or asking you to get into groups. This may take place in a taught session or via email. You may find that you have been placed with a group with students that you have never met before, and for some people this can be a daunting experience.

Table 8.2 Developing your group work skills

Behaviour	Place a tick in the relevant row each time you demonstrate that specific behaviour
Supporting each other	
Listening to other students by giving them your full attention	
Encouraging each other	
Helping the flow	
Making suggestions	
Giving praise	
Being honest	
Admitting mistakes	
Sharing information and ideas	
Working cooperatively	
Being prepared to compromise	
Giving constructive criticism	
Dealing with disagreements constructively by clarifying your understanding	
Providing summaries	
Keeping promises	

It is often best if one student takes the initiative and suggests a date, time and place to meet. It is always best to meet on 'neutral' territory (e.g., library or an on campus cafe) rather than in one person's home. It is best not to meet in locations such as a bar as this may not fit in with some students' religious beliefs, as well as which this type of environment is not conducive to study.

Once you have met it is important to get to know each other, so spend time on this. If you are working in an international team with members who have been educated in different countries then it is often helpful to talk about your previous experiences of group work. Some members may have had limited or no prior experience of assessed group work. If this is the case then you will all need to spend time talking about how to work together. Exchange contact information (e.g., names, email address, mobile and land line phone numbers). Talk about your expectations of the group work – how often do you want to meet;

what you will do if someone cannot attend; how you will record meetings; whether you want to nominate someone as group leader or coordinator.

You may also find it helpful to consider how to deal with problems in the group (see later in this chapter). It is worth thinking about what you will do if the group decides to break up. On some courses this is not allowed and once established a group has to work through until the end of the task. It is worth being clear about whether or not you are allowed to break up as a group. One common issue is if someone has all the data, information and references collected by the group and they don't make it available to other group members. One method of circumventing this potential problem is to ensure that every member uploads their data, information or references on a shared virtual learning environment. This means that if one or two students disappear from the group of if the group splits up then everyone still has access to the group's resources.

Next, spend some time focusing on your task and what is required. Look at the task details (e.g., in your module or course handbook) and make sure that you understand what is required and the deadline for handing in or presenting the work. Make sure you understand the assessment criteria and how individual and/ or group marks are allocated. Here are some common methods of assessing group work:

- All participating students obtain the same mark, i.e., the mark for the group product(s) is the same as individual marks
- Students are assigned marks according to a system, e.g., total participation leads to an individual mark which is the same as the mark received by the group, minimal participation leads to a mark of 40% (or the group mark if that is lower than 40%); and zero participation leads to a mark of 0%
- Students decide how much effort each student has contributed to the group product and individual student marks are then scaled up or down depending on the percentage effort recorded for each student
- Each student receives a mark for the shared group product and also an individual mark for an individual reflective commentary on the group process
- Each student's contribution to the final group product is clearly identified and they receive a mark for their contribution only.

As you can imagine, marking group work can become complicated. It is therefore important to understand the assessment requirements and how marks will be allocated for the group work at an early stage in the process.

You may then want to work out an action plan and agree key dates (e.g., for completing research, producing a first draft, editing, finalizing hand in or presentation details). As a group, you will need to decide who is going to do which part of the task and also how you are going to keep a record of your work. Remember to allow time for unexpected events such as someone being ill or difficulties in printing out your work. You will also need to arrange the date, time and location of the next meeting.

There are standard methods of organizing meetings in the workplace which help to make sure that the meeting is productive and there is no time wasted. Many lecturers encourage their students to use these standard practices as this means that you gain skills relevant to the workplace. When organizing group meetings it is important to:

- Make sure that everyone knows when and where the meeting is going to take place. Ask one person to act as leader or chairperson. Their job is to make sure that the meeting is organized in a business like manner, everyone contributes to the meeting, it keeps to time and decisions are made. This leadership role may be rotated, with a different person taking it on for each meeting or one person may take on the role for the whole task
- Agree an agenda (or list of topics for discussion) either before the meeting or at the start
- Discuss each topic on the agenda. Don't spend too long on any one topic. If necessary decide how long you will spend on each topic
- Make decisions! The purpose of the meeting is normally to share information and ideas, and then to make decisions
- Record these decisions. Ask one person to act as secretary and their role is to make notes of the meeting and its decisions. As with the leader or chairperson's role, the job of secretary can be rotated for each meeting or one person may take on the role for duration of the group task
- Decide when and where you will next meet. Most student groups find it best to have a regular meeting slot
- Write up the minutes or action notes of the meeting. These don't need to be long but they will help everyone to know how the group work is progressing
- This record is also useful if there is confusion or conflict within the group.

Example notes from a meeting

Research Methods Module: Group 32
Meeting on 12 February 2009. 11.15 BJL

Present: Tom, Bushra, Sam, Jane, Anne, Muhammid

Apologies: Takako (hospital appointment)

1 Notes of last meeting – everyone agreed with them.

2   Research – everyone reported their progress. Takako had sent a note in an email. The topic appears to be too big. Suggested that we focus on 3 instead of 6 countries (UK, India and China). Everyone agreed. **Action:** Anne to inform Takako.

3   Producing 1st draft. Muhammid suggested that everyone produced 250 words on their topic. He would put it together into one document and add an introduction and conclusion – agreed. Bushra said that she would then sort out references. Anne offered to read through whole document and edit it so that it read as one piece of work. This was agreed. **Action:** Everyone to have their 250 words to Muhammid by 11 February. Anne to inform Takako. Muhammid offered to have 1st draft ready for 15 February.

4   PowerPoint presentation. Decided to leave this until 1st draft produced.

5   Referencing. Some confusion about how to reference websites. **Action:** Bushra to email tutor.

6   Next tutorial. There is one booked for 14 February at 3 pm. Main issues: topic being too big. **Action:** Everyone to meet up at 2.50.

7   Next meeting: 15 February at 11.15 in BJL. **Action:** Tom will book room.

8   Notes of this meeting: **Action:** Jane to write up and email to everyone by Sunday.

It is a good idea to keep a record of your meetings and, in particular, who attended them, decisions made and action plans. These notes may become useful if there is a difference of opinion in the group (e.g., on different people's level of participation in the group work). On some modules or courses, you may be asked to hand in the minutes or notes from your group meetings as part of the assessment process.

One of the reasons for using group work is to enable you to learn from the experience and ideas about experiential learning are covered in Chapter 4. One of the best ways of learning from this experience is to review and reflect on your group work. Indeed, the assessment criteria for assessed group work often include an element of reflection or review. The process of identifying and spending some time reviewing group work is likely to be repaid as you and the group will learn to become reflective and learn from your successes and weaknesses.

The following questions may be used as prompts for reviewing group work:

1   Did you achieve your objectives?
2   Did you produce work to the required standards?
3   What were your main successes/failures?
4   In what areas did you not achieve your objectives?

5 Did working as a group help or hinder the achievement of your objectives?
6 Did you produce better or worse work as a result of working in the group?
7 How effective was the group in working together?
8 Did the group help and support individuals in their work?
9 What were the main strengths and weaknesses of group work?
10 How could you improve our outcomes?
11 How could you improve group working?
12 What are the main learning points for next time?

Activity 8.2 How well do you chair meetings?

The aim of this activity is to help you to develop meeting skills and leadership skills. Group work provides students with an opportunity to develop leadership skills and an important skill is the ability to chair or coordinate meetings. This activity will help you to reflect on your ability to chair meetings. Look at Table 8.3 which outlines positive behaviours and score yourself (0 = never, 10 = always). Alternatively, you may ask a friend to complete the score sheet for you. Once you have obtained the results from the checklist, reflect on them. Identify the areas where you score highly. Identify areas for improvement. You may find it helpful to use this information to consider how you will improve the quality of the next meeting that you chair.

Working in diverse groups

A major advantage of group work is that it enables different people to work together and share their ideas, perspectives and experiences. Nowadays the work-force in organizations is very diverse as people from different backgrounds and countries work together. The ability to work in a diverse group is an important skill and essential for working in a global economy. During your programme of studies you are likely to work in diverse groups and this is a great opportunity for broadening your experience and perspectives. Sometimes it can be a challenging experience and lead to some feelings of discomfort. It is a great opportunity for learning and developing your communication and group work skills.

Working in a diverse group normally involves more effort than working in a group where everyone comes from the same background and has a similar perspective. It is particularly important to spend time getting to know each other, learning each other's names (and how they are pronounced correctly) and talking about your expectations of group work. Students coming to business schools or departments come from many different educational backgrounds and

Table 8.3 How well do you chair meetings?

Do you . . .	Never										Always
Make sure that you have prepared and circulated the right documents	0	1	2	3	4	5	6	7	8	9	10
Think through the different agenda items and how individuals might respond to them	0	1	2	3	4	5	6	7	8	9	10
Keep to time	0	1	2	3	4	5	6	7	8	9	10
Keep the discussions on topic	0	1	2	3	4	5	6	7	8	9	10
Ask quiet team members for their thoughts	0	1	2	3	4	5	6	7	8	9	10
Manage dominant members	0	1	2	3	4	5	6	7	8	9	10
Deal with difficult topics in a sensitive manner	0	1	2	3	4	5	6	7	8	9	10
Give others the chance to speak	0	1	2	3	4	5	6	7	8	9	10
Explain your reasons for disagreement	0	1	2	3	4	5	6	7	8	9	10
Listen to the viewpoints of others even when you disagree with them	0	1	2	3	4	5	6	7	8	9	10
Prevent the meeting from getting bogged down in too much detail	0	1	2	3	4	5	6	7	8	9	10
Prevent general moaning sessions	0	1	2	3	4	5	6	7	8	9	10
Follow up if you agree to take action	0	1	2	3	4	5	6	7	8	9	10
Ensure that the notes from the meeting are written up and circulated within a reasonable time period	0	1	2	3	4	5	6	7	8	9	10

countries and they will have different experiences of group work – some students may have never been involved in group work before. Cameron (2005:237) writes:

> Working in mixed groups takes more effort. It becomes even more vital to check understanding at every stage than it is with a homogenous group. Words mean slightly different things within different cultures. Some cultures are less assertive than others: their 'agreement' may be mere politeness. Some cultures express themselves very directly, in ways that may

seem almost offensive to others but are just the 'normal' way of saying things to those concerned. Some cultures treat deadlines differently from others.

The general advice for working in diverse groups is to:

• Meet in a place which is acceptable to everyone and that is 'neutral' territory
• Make sure you know each other's names
• Spend time getting to know each other
• Make sure that everyone has a chance to speak.
• Ask quiet members for their opinions
• Include everyone and ask for individuals' comments
• Check understanding and use of terminology
• Check agreement
• Make sure that there is a common understanding about deadlines.

An important skill in cross-cultural working is to be open and upfront about different ways of working and communicating with each other. If you are working in a group with students from other cultures and you think that there are some underlying cross-cultural issues then talk about them. This will give you the opportunity to learn from each other and become more skilled in working in diverse groups.

Up to 10 percent of students in higher education have a disability and these may be visible, (e.g., limited mobility or a visual impairment) or they may be invisible (e.g., dyslexia or mental health issues such as obsessive compulsive disorder). You may have a disability yourself. Some students with disabilities gain additional help and support from the university or college disability services, while other students will keep their personal situation private. Sometimes a student's disability may limit their ability to take part in group work and, if you find yourself in this situation, it might be worthwhile talking about it and finding out how the student can best contribute to the group work. This type of conversation is likely to be a sensitive one so it is probably best to hold it in private rather than in front of the whole group. If you find yourself working in a group where either your own disability or that of another student begins to affect adversely the group process it is normally a good idea to talk about it in a sensitive way or to ask for advice from your tutor or the disability services. However, it is worth remembering that with the majority of students who have disabilities this will not affect their ability to work in groups.

Virtual groups

Many business and management students will find themselves working in virtual groups at some stage in their programme of study. Students who are attending a programme on campus may find it difficult to meet up with each other (e.g., because of timetabling pressures or part time employment). In addition, some programmes may involve students who are living and working across the world and virtual group work offers an important way of enhancing the student learning experience. Virtual group work may involve using email, videophones, online discussion groups and chat or conferencing. Some groups never meet face to face, while others may meet once or twice during the life of the group. Multinational organizations now rely on virtual group work as a means of communicating across countries and as a way of managing particular problems or issues. This means that if you develop the skills in working in virtual groups or teams it will be valued by future employers.

One common strategy for circumventing geographic and time constraints is to work in virtual groups using online communication tools such as email, discussion or bulletin boards and conference or chat rooms. While working in virtual groups gives individual members the opportunity to access their group at a time and place that suits them, it also raises some challenges to group work. How do you develop trust and confidence in the group and its members if you have never met them? How do you take into account the different cultural backgrounds of students from a wide range of countries?

Working together in face to face groups gives individuals the opportunity to size each other up, get to know each other's work style, habits and preferences, and build relationships. In particular, sitting around a table means that you gain immediate feedback from someone's replies (or silences) and their body language. In contrast virtual group working involves communicating with other group members through text (in the case of email, discussion groups or conference rooms) sometimes with the support of video streamed images (e.g., when video-conferencing).

The five step model based on the work of Gilly Salmon (2000) and adapted here provides a helpful outline of the key stages in virtual group work. This model is presented in Table 8.4.

In order to encourage an effective virtual group here are some examples of the types of activities that online group coordinators may facilitate:

Stage 1: Access and motivation

- Ensure that the online group or thread is set up with a welcome message
- Ensure group members know how to access the online group
- Chase up absent members

Table 8.4 Five step model of virtual group work

Stage	Group member activities
Stage 1: access and motivation	Entering the virtual environment Finding your way around Experimenting with the system Asking for technical help
Stage 2: online socialization	Getting to know each other Sharing information about yourself Starting to develop a group culture
Stage 3: information exchange	Sharing ideas Exploring roles and responsibilities Allocating project tasks Initial research Reporting and discussing findings
Stage 4: producing the required products	Carrying out activities Helping each other Giving and receiving feedback Problem solving Completing group tasks
Stage 5: closure	Complete all group tasks Complete review and evaluation processes Goodbyes

Stage 2: Online socialization

- Lead a round of introductions
- Welcome new group members or late arrivals
- Provide a structure for getting started, e.g., agreement of group rules
- If individuals break the agreed ground rules, tackle them (either privately or through the discussion group)
- Wherever possible avoid playing 'ping pong' with individual group members and ask other people for their opinions and ideas
- Encourage quieter group members to join in
- Provide summaries of online discussions.

Stage 3: Information exchange

- Share ideas
- Explore and allocate roles and responsibilities
- Allocate project tasks
- Organize initial research

- Encourage members to report and discuss initial findings
- Encourage participation
- Invite quiet members to participate
- Chase up absent members
- Ask questions
- Give praise
- Encourage group members to post short messages
- Encourage reflection.

Stage 4: Producing the required product

- Coordinate the different project activities
- Encourage members to help each other
- Encourage members to give and receive feedback
- Encourage problem solving
- Monitor process with respect to project plan
- Facilitate the process
- Ensure that the group completes its task
- Ask questions
- Give praise
- Encourage reflection.

Stage 5: Closure

- Ensure 'loose ends' are completed
- Highlight group achievements
- Encourage (structured) reflection and evaluation on group process
- Thank group members for their contributions and work
- Formally close the project.

Common problems in group work

Table 8.5 outlines some common problems in group work and different strategies for managing them. Working in student groups is similar to working in groups in organisations. People vary in how much effort they put into their work and this is sometimes a cause of frustration and conflict within a group. Learning how to deal with these situations in the university environment will help you to develop leadership skills for the workplace.

Table 8.5 Common problems in group work

Problem	Strategy for managing it
Student doesn't attend or make contact via email or text message	Keep contacting the student and inviting them to meetings Inform your tutor Use meeting notes / minutes to demonstrate attendance and participation
Some students may want to take over and dominate group work. They may want to hold meetings at their house/room, be the group leader, and control the group work	Strategies for managing this include: meeting on neutral territory, sharing leadership and coordination roles by taking turns, making sure that everyone has a turn. You may find it useful to talk to each other about the best ways of working together and sharing the work
Students who don't commit to the group work or are only aiming for a low mark	This can be very frustrating. It is worth talking about it in the group and deciding how you are going to organize yourselves and work together. You may also want to raise it as a group issue. If you have a choice over assignment title then choose a topic that everyone is interested in. The marking of some group assignments takes into account different levels of participation
Free-loader: the person who doesn't do any work or turns up the week before an assignment is due to be handed in and then wants to get involved	Another awkward situation. Your meeting notes/minutes will enable you to demonstrate attendance and levels of activity. The marking of some group assignments takes into account different levels of participation. If a student doesn't contribute to group work it is appropriate for the group to inform the tutor. There may be some reason(s) for nonparticipation and, if this is the case, the student concerned should inform the tutor of the reason(s)
Conflict between group members	Occasionally conflict does arise between group members. It is worth remembering that conflict may lead to extremely creative and high quality work. However, it sometimes results in uncomfortable and awkward situations. Strategies for dealing with conflict include: having a cooling off period; discussing the situation and ways of resolving it; building on common ground and agreement; asking another person to mediate

Managing the emotional aspects of group work

Working in groups is sometimes an emotional experience as shown by the following comments from students:

> I was put into a group by the tutor and there was one person I found annoying. I was constantly irritated by her but had to put up with it.

> I found it very stressful. I got really angry in some of the meetings but held my tongue to preserve the peace. One of the other students was very aggressive and constantly put me down. She made my life hell. It only began to improve when we asked the tutor for help.

> At first I was very nervous about working with the others. I'd never worked with people from other countries before. Once we got to know each other it got easier. We became friends and at the end of the Unit we went out for a Chinese meal together. We still see each other. In hindsight it was a great way of making us to get to know other students and become friends.

> It was a roller coaster of highs (the actual presentation, finishing the project) and lows (no-one replying to my emails, Charlie and Anya falling out, Sam not completing his section). I was relieved when it was over but I did learn a lot.

Cottrell (1999) describes some of the strong emotions that appear in group work and she divides them into three main categories:

- *Differences in opinions*. Sometimes different group members will hold strong opinions and emotions may be aroused if these are not mentioned or if they are dealt with in a confrontational or judgemental way. It is worth remembering that it is acceptable to challenge opinions but *not* to attack the person who holds the opinion
- *Group problems*, e.g., individuals may feel left out or excluded, they may feel

that some members are not pulling their weight or they may feel that someone is dominating the group. If you identify that your group has this type of problem then it is normally best to raise it in a nonconfrontational way, e.g., 'Shall we let everyone say what they think about that idea' or 'I think we need to share the work out more equally so that everyone has a fair share'

- *External problems*. Sometimes individiuals will bring to meetings problems that have nothing to do with the group. For example, they may have fallen out with their boyfriend or girlfriend and bring their distress to the group. If this happens it is worthwhile giving the student a chance to talk about the issue so that they 'get if off their chest' and then return the focus to the group task.

Sometimes situations arise in groups that result in tears. If this happens with someone in your group it is normally best to let the student cry as this helps release stress. Ask them if they want a break or if they want to speak to a friend for a few minutes. Remember to be kind and supportive. If a group member constantly cries then there may be a serious underlying problem in which case it may be helpful to take advice from your tutor.

Another issue that sometimes arises is if another student gets angry and shouts or behaves in an aggressive manner. If this happens it is normally best to let them cool down (e.g., by taking a break), and then resuming the group work. Aggressive behaviour is unacceptable and if necessary take advice from your tutor as to how to deal with the issue.

Finally, another approach to handling the emotional aspects of group work is by thinking about the concept of emotional intelligence which is described in Chapter 2.

Summary

Group skills are essential for working in different types of organizations. Effective groups are well organized, spend time building up relationships and have good quality communications. Working in diverse groups gives all students the opportunity to learn from people with different experiences and perspectives. Finally, most groups experience difficulties or challenges at some point and by working to overcome these issues you will develop the skills required to work in global organizations.

9

Professional experience and study abroad

Introduction • Professional experience • Study abroad • Assessing the professional or study abroad experiences • Summary

Introduction

The aim of this chapter is to provide you with guidance on professional experience and international opportunities or study abroad. An increasing number of business and management students take part in professional experience (through work placements), on study abroad or international experiences as a means of developing their knowledge and skills, and enhancing their CV. Students who return from a professional experience or study abroad experience often say that the experience has helped them to mature, increase their self-confidence and become more independent. In addition, the experience helps them to 'stand out' in the job market.

This chapter is divided into four sections: professional experience; study abroad; assessing the professional experience or study abroad experiences; and returning to studies.

Professional experience

Many students take up the opportunity to enrol on a business and management degree programme that provides an opportunity for a professional experience placement, sometimes called a work placement. These are normally built into the programme and last for one or two semesters and/or vacations. They are normally credit rated, in other words there will be an associated assessment activity which counts towards your final degree results. In addition to these formal professional experiences that are integrated into the programme, many students become involved in professional or work experience opportunities or internships during the vacations. If you are thinking of taking part in a period of professional experience Table 9.1 presents some of the advantages and disadvantages identified by students who have just returned from their 'year at work'.

If you are interested in taking up the opportunity to have a professional experience placement then your department or business school will help prepare and

Table 9.1 Advantages and disadvantages of the professional experience

Advantages	Disadvantages
• Gained real life work experience • Discovered that I could make a difference in the workplace • Improved my IT skills • Obtained a job for when I graduate • Put theory into practice. All the stuff we had studied on the course suddenly made much better sense • Earned a lot of money • Had the opportunity to live and work in London • Discovered that I didn't want to work in a business. I'm now thinking of working in the voluntary sector • Gained confidence • Gained experience of working in a company with offices and customers all around the world • Travelled around the UK and EU as part of my job • Improved my motivation • I met some great people • Enhanced my *curriculum vitae*.	• Even though I got help in looking for a work placement I had to make more than 30 applications before I was successful • It took me a while to settle in my job. People were friendly but I missed my uni friends • Some of my friends will graduate before me and we won't be in the final year together • My first work placement was a disaster and they were using me as cheap labour. I told my tutor and after a bit of hassle I got a new placement. The new company is great • I had to work and do some uni work. I found it hard writing up the work placement report but it did help me get back into my studies • I had to pay fees during the year out *but* they were reduced • It took me a while to settle back into my studies in the final year.

support you for the experience. The detailed arrangements will vary but they are likely to start at least a year before the placement and may include the following:

- Briefing sessions that introduce the professional experience or work placement and outline the arrangements to support students. You will have an opportunity to discuss the benefits and challenges involved in undertaking a placement and also how it is likely to make an impact on your future career. You will be able to hear from students who have returned from a placement
- Information on how to find a placement and advertisements of suitable professional experience opportunities. There is likely to be a virtual placement site where vacancies are posted here as they are received. This site may include external links to websites providing access to information related to placements and career management. Alternatively, this information may be available via the careers service
- Preparatory workshops on topics such as: finding a placement, writing your *curriculum vitae*, making a positive impact at interviews, writing up the placement experience in an assessed report
- Tutorial support from a placement tutor whose role may include the following:
  - To provide you with support before and during your placement experience
  - To visit you at your placement
  - To help you achieve your placement goals and learning objectives
  - To help you deal with any challenging situations you may experience during the placement
  - To advise you on the assessment requirements of the placement
  - To write reports on their visits to you
  - To assess any work that is associated with your placement.

Students with a disability

If you have a disability then specialist staff in your college or university will be able to provide you with advice and support on how to gain the maximum benefit from your placement year. They will be able to help you prepare for your placement in areas such as:

- How to disclose a disability to prospective employers
- Discussing additional equipment needs or adaptations required with employers
- Negotiating reasonable adjustments while on placement
- Accessing financial assistance for any additional equipment required during a placement.

A site which may also be of interest to you is www.skill.org.uk (the National Bureau for Students with Disabilities).

International students

If you are an international student and you wish to take up a professional experience placement opportunity then you will need to ensure that you have a relevant work permit. The rules and regulations concerning work permits are complex and they change regularly. Your university or college will be able to provide you with relevant information. Useful sources of information include the websites: www.workpermit.com and www.workignintheuk.gov.uk

What do you want to gain from a professional experience placement?

If you are thinking about obtaining professional experience then it is worthwhile spending a little time thinking about what you want to gain from the experience and also how it will fit into your career plans. The following are some questions that will help you clarify your requirements.

What sort of professional experience will fit into your degree programme?

The purpose of obtaining professional experience is to allow you to integrate knowledge and skills gained during the earlier stages of your studies with real life work experience. This means that your work placement should be relevant to your course of study and provide a practical learning experience for you. Some general factors you should take into account include:

- The sector and organizational environment. You will need to think about which sector you want to work in, e.g., retail, financial and also your preferred type of organization, e.g., multinational, small or medium sized enterprise, public sector, voluntary sector
- The actual professional experience or job role(s). Do you want to gain experience within a particular department, e.g., marketing? Or do you want your experience to be very broad and include a wide range of departments or functions? Do you want your experience to count towards professional accreditation?
- The levels of responsibility that you will be given. Will you have opportunities to take on responsibilities, e.g., managing a project?
- The variety of duties and/or projects. In general, the more varied the experience that you obtain the greater value it will be to your future career and employers. Some organizations offer professional experience placements where you will have the opportunity to obtain experience of working in a number of different departments
- Opportunities for staff development and training. Staff development and

training is a useful way of developing your professional practice. Some work placements will count towards professional accreditation and your employer may help you prepare for their examinations
- The levels of support provided within the organization. Many organizations provide extremely structured professional experience placements for students who, in addition to a line manager, are provided with a workplace mentor and opportunities to reflect on and integrate their professional experiences into their academic knowledge and future career plans. In other situations, support may be limited to that provided by their workplace manager. It is important that the organization is committed to taking a professional experience placement student and that they provide you with appropriate support and encouragement. Your new employer needs to understand that in addition to working for them as an employee you are there to develop yourself and your career. This means that they need to take time to explain workplace issues or activities to you
- Finally, it is really important that you obtain a professional experience 'placement' rather than a 'job'. The main purpose of the professional experience opportunity on degree programmes is to enable you to develop your professional skills and to integrate academic knowledge with workplace practices.

Where do you want to go?

Students who gain the most from their professional experience placements are those who are open minded and flexible about where they are willing to work. Limiting yourself to a particular geographical location will limit the workplace opportunities that are open to you. If you are open minded and willing to consider a wide range of work placement options in different locations then you will find you are able to choose from a range of fantastic opportunities. The experience of moving to a new town or country and settling into a new lifestyle will also help you to develop new life skills. Many employers are looking for flexible and independent graduates who can stand on their own two feet. One of the advantages of being adventurous in your choice of work placement is that you will have back-up from your tutor and department or business school and they will provide you will help and support if you come across challenging situations. Students who have been on professional experience placements report that they soon settle down in their new environment and make a new set of friends starting with their workplace colleagues. Here are some comments from students:

My work placement was in London and I found a flat sharing with an old school friend. It was great. I soon made a new circle of friends. The work placement was very good and I gained lots of useful experience. The company has offered me work in my holidays.

I moved to Paris. At first it was strange and a bit difficult then I made friends with another English girl at work and we found a good flat. My social life began to develop and I now have friends from all over Europe. The job was good and very interesting. It was in an English-speaking office but I found my French improved. I recommend a work placement in another country. It is like having a gap year with pay.

Finding a professional experience placement

As indicated earlier in this chapter, your business school, department, university or college will provide you with help in finding a professional experience placement. In addition to the help and support that they provide students seeking work placements, you may also want to search out your own placement. This is likely to involve carrying out research, making speculative approaches to organizations or networking (e.g., at career fairs, seminars or conferences, or at events organized by professional bodies). It is impossible for your university or college to provide you with information about every single placement opportunity that exists. You may increase your chances of securing a placement by:

- Searching the Internet and looking at useful websites such as:
  ○ www.work-experience.org
  ○ www.step.prg.uk
  ○ www.placements.org
  ○ www.internetjobs.com
  ○ www.enhanceuk.com
  ○ www.fledglings.net
  ○ www.thegraduate.co.uk
- Identifying individual organizations and then sending a speculative letter
- Attending careers fairs and marketing yourself
- Networking, e.g., by attending events organized by your department, business school or professional bodies; making use of your family and friends' networks.

Each year thousands of business and management students are searching for professional experience placements and there is a high level of competition. This means that you must be proactive and you may need to apply for more than 30 positions before you are successful. If you find that you are not successful, for example you are repeatedly turned down after interviews, then contact your tutor and ask for advice. It may be that you need to develop and improve your interview skills and you will be helped in this by your department, business school or careers service.

It is important that you keep detailed records of your applications. The easiest way to do this is to keep a file and for each position to keep a copy of the job advertisement/description and your application. You will need to refer to these should an employer invite you to an interview. Keep a printed record of all your communications with the company plus information that you have obtained in your research on the company. This is really important as it will help you in your preparations for interviews. It will also help prevent you from confusing the different applications.

What happens when you are on your professional experience placement?

During your professional experience placement you will be treated as an employee and this means that you need to behave in a professional manner, fit into the culture of the organization, and follow its policies and procedures. You will also need to be on time for work and fit in with the requirements of the organization's working day. If the organization has a dress code then you will need to follow it. You will be asked to attend an induction programme and this will help you to become familiar with the organization. You will have a manager or supervisor who will provide you with guidance on what is expected in the workplace. In addition, you may be provided with a mentor who will provide you with general support and career guidance.

What happens if things go wrong? Sometimes problems do arise during a professional experience/work placement. Students may be asked to work extremely long hours, in dangerous conditions or to carry out tasks that are not at the appropriate level (e.g., spend all day making tea and photocopying). If you experience problems, first talk to your manager or supervisor to see if the issue can be sorted out informally. If this doesn't resolve the situation then make contact with the human resources or personnel department, or contact your tutor or personal supervisor. Remember the aim of the work placement is to enable you to obtain appropriate experience to enhance your knowledge, skills and career prospects. If this is not happening then it is important to inform the appropriate people. If you don't know what to do about a particularly challenging situation then contact your tutor.

Study abroad

There is an increasing number of opportunities for business and management students to take part in international or study abroad experiences. This experience provides an important opportunity for you to broaden your horizons and develop your knowledge of international business and management, and political and economic issues. In addition, the experience will help you to develop your skills in living and working in another culture as well as working in intercultural teams. Many businesses and other organizations (e.g., government services and development agencies) actively seek employees who have had experience of living and either studying or working abroad.

Study abroad or international experiences are normally built into individual degree programmes and they typically last for one or two semesters. They are normally credit rated, in other words there will be an associated assessment activity which counts towards your final degree results. In addition to study abroad experiences that are integrated into the programme, many students become involved in international summer schools, which are a means of spending a shorter period living and studying in another country.

If you are thinking of taking part in a study abroad or international experience Table 9.2 presents some of the advantages and disadvantages identified by students who have just returned from their study abroad.

If you are interested in taking up the opportunity to have a work or study abroad experience your department or business school will help prepare and support you for the experience. There is likely to be an work or study abroad coordinator (or office) who will provide you with help and support, and act as a source of information and support. Many departments or business schools provide a specialist study abroad website. The detailed arrangements for studying abroad will vary but they are likely to include the following:

- Information and briefing sessions that outline the arrangements to support students and enable you to discuss the benefits and challenges involved in undertaking study abroad
- Opportunities to meet students who have completed a study abroad experience
- Information on the range of international experiences that are available. Many universities and colleges will have formal arrangements with partner institutions in other countries. These arrangements make it easier to take part in international experience as they are likely to be well organized and professionally run
- Opportunities to meet staff from the host university. Sometimes these opportunities are arranged face to face and at other times via videoconferencing

Table 9.2 Advantages and disadvantages of the study abroad or international experience

Advantages	Disadvantages
<ul><li>I now understand what globalization and internationalization are all about</li><li>Gained real life experience of living in another country</li><li>Learnt how to live and work with people from lots of different cultures</li><li>Gained experience of working in cross-cultural teams</li><li>Improved my language skills – French</li><li>Gained a different perspective on the world</li><li>Made friends from around the world</li><li>Gained confidence</li><li>Improved my motivation</li><li>I met some great people</li><li>Spent three months travelling around the USA at the end of the university year</li><li>Enhanced my *curriculum vitae*</li></ul>	<ul><li>It was scary at first</li><li>It took me some time to work out the way things worked in my host university</li><li>It took me a while to settle into my studies</li><li>I missed my uni friends</li><li>I missed my family</li><li>Some of my friends will graduate before me and we won't be in the final year together</li></ul>

- Access to a virtual learning site that contains information about recommended study abroad opportunities. Alternatively, this information may be available via the careers service. Some useful sites include:
  - http://www.studyabroad.com/guides/handbook/handbook4.html
  - http://www.worldwide.edu/travel_planner/culture_shock.html
  - http://www.esl-lab.com/shock1/shock1.htm#pre
  - http://www.internationalstudent.com/
  - http://www.aec.ku.edu/counselors/corner.html
- Preparatory workshops on topics such as: selecting an international experience, the application process, studying abroad, assessment activities, working in inter-cultural teams, living abroad
- Tutorial support from an experienced tutor whose role may include the following:
  - To provide you with support before and during your study abroad experience
  - To visit you during your international experience
  - To help you achieve your international experience goals and learning objectives
  - To help you deal with any challenging situations you may experience during your international experience
  - To advise you on the assessment requirements of the international experience
  - To write reports on their visits to you.

Students with a disability

If you have a disability then specialist staff in your college or university will be able to provide you with advice and support on how to gain the maximum benefit from your international experience. They will be able to help you prepare for your international experience in areas such as:

• Discussing additional equipment needs or adaptations required with the host institution
• Negotiating reasonable adjustments during your study abroad experience
• Accessing financial assistance for any additional equipment required during your international experience.

A site which may also be of interest to you is www.skill.org.uk (the National Bureau for Students with Disabilities).

What do you want to gain from an international experience?

If you are thinking about studying abroad then it is worth spending a little time thinking about what you want to gain from the experience and how it will fit into your career plans. Here are some questions that will help you clarify your requirements:

• How will the study abroad experience fit into my career plans? Do I want to work in a particular country when I graduate? Do I need to develop certain language skills to enhance my career?
• Where do I want to live and study? You need to think about the country and university or college. In addition, think about whether you want to experience living in a capital city, a large or a small town
• How long do I want to study abroad? Is it one semester, an academic year, a summer school or some other period?
• How will this experience fit into my programme of study? How will I be able to study modules or courses that fit into my career plans? What are the implications for gaining professional accreditation? Is my host institution accredited by the relevant accrediting bodies?
• What language is used to teach in the host university? Will I be able to improve my language skills? Will I be able to learn new languages? How is this experience assessed?
• Will I be able to gain academic credit for this experience?
• Will I be able to learn about businesses and other organizations in the host country, e.g., by visits, guest speakers or short periods of work experience?

Practical arrangements

Your business school or department will provide you with extensive information through briefing and workshop sessions, and also via a website. Staff from the host institutions may come to talk to prospective students and you may have the opportunity to talk to returning students. You need to think about the following topics.

Application form

You will need to apply for a place to study at the host institution. The first stage is to complete their application form either on paper or online. As with applying for a job, you will need to complete the application form promptly and meet the host institution's deadlines. The amount of detail required to complete this form varies from university to university, and department to department. In addition to the completed form, some institutions require additional documentation, e.g., transcript of grades, a reference and medical certificates. In some countries you need to be able to demonstrate that you have been vaccinated against certain diseases and you will need to provide vaccination certificates. It is important to allow plenty of time to complete these requirements. In addition, you may be asked to provide financial information or guarantees. This may involve providing copies of saving account statements, a letter from your parents (with a supporting statement from their bank) and a letter from your local education authority, sponsor or student loan company confirming your financial status. Your department or business school will provide you with help on how to complete the application form and organize the associated documentation.

Passports and visas

You will require an up to date passport and you will need to ensure that it does not expire during your study abroad period. Check the requirements for the country well in advance of your study abroad period. Visas are not required for every country and requirements can change from year to year. You may need a visa to enter the country as a student and/or for residency reasons. You may also need a visa if you intend to work in the country. Staff in your university or college will advise you on whether or not you need a visa and on the visa application process. You are advised to fill out your passport and visa forms as far in advance as possible and, as with the application form, you will need to provide detailed information in order to gain your visa. If you do not provide the required information or if you fill in the forms incorrectly the process of gaining your passport or visa will be delayed. You are likely to be asked to provide your passport with the application form and the whole process may take six weeks or more. This means that you should avoid any holiday plans during this period. If you post the application and associated documentation including your passport make sure that you use recorded delivery or a reliable messenger service. Alternatively, you may visit the relevant embassy or visa office and queue for your visa. This may involve many hours of standing in one or more queues and it is important to have the correct documentation with all the relevant papers correctly completed. It is extremely frustrating to queue all day and then find that your application has been turned down as you have not provided all the correct information or supporting documents. Most embassies and visa offices have websites and these provide information about obtaining your visa and the amount of time it is likely to take.

It is sometimes possible to fast track your passport and/or visa application but this is likely to involve visiting the relevant offices and spending a long time in queues. It is also likely to involve an additional administration fee.

Money

You will need to sort out your finances before you start your study abroad period. In terms of money you will need to think about:

- Costs of studying abroad
  - Application fee – this may be returnable
  - Administrative fees
  - Tuition fees (these may be payable to your home or host institution)
- Accommodation
  - Rent plus costs such as electricity, heat, local authority fees
  - Housing deposits
  - Food
- Travel
  - Travel between your home country and the host country
  - Travel within your host country. Rail travel is often cheap and affordable using special student discounts
  - Travel costs to attend lectures and classes
  - Leisure and social travel costs
- Travel documents
  - Passport fee
  - Visa fee
  - Cost of medical immunizations
  - International student identity card
- Insurance
  - Travel insurance
  - Medical insurance

- Study needs
  - Textbooks
  - Field trips
  - Stationery
  - Computer consumables
  - Printing
- Personal expenses
  - Mobile phone
  - Personal care products
  - Laundry
  - Additional clothes
  - Social life
  - Sports activities.

You will need to be aware that exchange rates vary, so if your finances are very limited and there is an adverse change in an exchange rate this could cause you major financial problems.

For European students, there are many grants available to help support your study abroad and your department or business school will be able to provide you with up to date information. These grants are available from various educational schemes within the European Union as well as national, regional or local funds. Staff in your university or college will advise you about sources of funding including scholarships for your international experience.

Scholarships provide a useful means of gaining additional funding. It is worthwhile considering applying for a scholarship as gaining one has a number of advantages, apart from the obvious financial advantage. Gaining a scholarship will enhance your *curriculum vitae*. As part of the scholarship, you may be asked to become involved in a variety of activities, for example acting as a student ambassador or representative, and you may receive special invitations to a number of different formal and informal functions. This will enrich your study abroad experience. It is worth remembering that each year some scholarships are not awarded due to a lack of applications. It is well worth spending time and effort applying for scholarships. The information that you have used in making your study abroad application will be useful in completing your scholarship application. It is likely that you will be asked to provide a personal statement as well as references.

Travel

There are many different travel options available to students (e.g., budget airlines, ferry, train and/or long distance coach). You will find that the rates are often competitive with very good deals for students. If you are travelling with friends it may be worthwhile exploring group travel options as these are often cheaper. In general, it is cheaper either to book well in advance or to use last minute deals. If you know that you will want to travel at peak times such as holiday periods then it is best to book well in advance as there may be very limited or no last minute deals. You will find that there are often grants available for air fares and other travel costs, and your university or college will advice you on how to apply for assistance.

Many students take the opportunity to travel in their host country or continent during or after their study abroad experience. They may travel at weekends, on public holidays or during the long vacation between the end of the study abroad experience and their return to their home institution. Many students use this time to travel with the friends that they have made during their study abroad experience and to visit each other's homes or to travel and work together in different places. This makes the travelling process less daunting and safer, as you will be travelling with friends. There are also many volunteering opportunities and some students combine travel, paid employment and volunteering. All of these experiences can be used to enhance your *curriculum vitae*.

Medical requirements

Medical requirements vary from country to country and your university or college will provide you with up to date advice. If you come from and are studying in an European Union country then you should be covered provided that you obtain the European Health Insurance Card (available via http://www.ehicard.org). If you are studying abroad in a non-European country then you will find that you are responsible for paying the costs of your medical care. This means that you *must* obtain medical insurance and you will not be able to register at your host university without it. Some universities insist that you take out a policy with their insurance company or they stipulate the criteria that must be covered by the insurance. You will need to organize your medical insurance before you set off. Your university or college will be able to provide you with help and support about medical matters including possible sources of funding.

In addition to insurance, you will have to provide authenticated medical records (i.e., all medical evidence has to be stamped and signed by your doctor). You will need to have proof that you have had all the required vaccinations, chest X-rays, blood tests, etc. You will be advised on the specific documentation that you need. Obtaining these certificates and additional vaccinations is becoming increasingly expensive. You will normally have to provide original certificates, and photocopies will not be accepted. If you do not have the required medical documentation then you may not be allowed to register at the university or move into student accommodation. This may delay the start of your study abroad period.

When you arrive at your host institution, it is important to find out how to register for a doctor and how to access medical and dental services. These topics are likely to be covered in induction. Tourist guides also provide this type of information. It is worthwhile knowing where to go in a medical emergency (e.g., the location of the local hospital, dentist and pharmacy). Different countries have different arrangements with respect to access to medical support and the roles of different specialists (e.g., pharmacists) vary from country to country. In some countries, you will find that there is a health centre or pharmacy available on-campus.

Accommodation

Many universities and colleges ensure that when they organize study abroad experiences for their students the arrangements include a guaranteed place in university accommodation. However, this is not always the case. In some countries, students may live in privately rented accommodation, student hostels or with a host family (particularly for summer schools). You will need to check with your university or college to find out what arrangements have been made concerning accommodation. You will also need to find out what is provided within the accommodation and what you will need to take with you. It is worthwhile finding out about the provision of:

- Pillows and duvets
- Sheets and other linen
- Cooking equipment
- Phones and computers.

In addition, it is worth talking to returning students who will have experienced accommodation in the host institution and who will be able to give you good advice. Some student flats and houses are passed on from one group of study abroad students to another.

You will find that there are different customs and practices concerning student accommodation. For example, in the UK student accommodation is normally in single rooms and these increasingly have ensuite facilities. In contrast, students in the USA often share a room with another student and these are called 'dorms'. Some universities and colleges have international halls or houses and these are reserved for students from around the world who are studying there. Selecting to live in an international hall provides you with a good opportunity to mix with a diverse group of students. Many students find it is best not to share accommodation with friends from their home university as this can make it more difficult to mix and make new friends. In many ways living with familiar faces is likely to reduce the impact and learning opportunities of your study abroad experience. In some countries, you may be expected to organize your own accommodation, for example in a rented flat or shared house, or students may be accommodated with host families. Again, your business school or department and returning students will be able to provide you with advice on accommodation.

If you are sharing a room with someone from a different culture then you may find some of their habits quite different to your own and vice versa. This sometimes causes tensions. The best advice is to be as open as possible with your roommate and to talk about living together and any different habits or customs. You may find it helpful to establish a few ground rules, for example about visitors and loud music. One of the advantages of sharing a room is that it is a good way of making friends and forming new social networks. In most institutions it is possible to change roommates if you really cannot get on together.

Weather

It is important to know something about the weather of the country that you will be studying in and how it varies as this helps you to know what clothes to take with you. Important information to obtain is the extremes of temperature during the summer and winter, and also the amount of rainfall. This information is readily available via the Internet. Alternatively, talk to returning students. This information will help you to be prepared and pack the right kind of clothes.

Your first few weeks

Being prepared

When you set out to your host university ensure that you have all relevant information (including emergency contact details) in your hand luggage. You are likely to be met at the local airport or train station, and escorted to your accommodation. If you are unsure about these arrangements then do check with your home institution before you leave. If you have the option of being met at the station or airport and making your own way to the university then it is advisable to take up the offer of the escort. This will mean that you immediately start meeting people in your host institution.

Induction

There is likely to be an induction day or week for all new international students. The content of the induction event will vary from institution to institution, but it is likely to include the following:

- Welcome
- Tour of campus
- Tour of local town
- General introduction to life at the university
- Introduction to your new department or school
- Introduction to the organization of your programme of study and the rules and regulations of the host college or university
- Social and cultural events.

Induction events are very, very important as they provide you with an opportunity to make friends, meet key staff and also begin to settle into your new college or university. In addition, these induction events help you become familiar with your new surroundings and to identify key buildings or venues. They provide a great opportunity to make new friends and they will help you to establish new friendship networks. Once teaching begins it is likely to become more challenging to make new friends as you will find that you have a very full timetable.

During the induction period you will also be given advice on practical aspects of living in your host country and this will cover topics such as bank accounts, obtaining employment, medical facilities, post boxes and obeying the law. If you are thinking about obtaining paid employment then it is a good idea to start looking as soon as you arrive at your host institution. International students often arrive a week earlier than other students and this will give you an advantage over the other students who will not arrive until after induction. Again, returning students will be able to provide you with advice on jobs before you leave your own country. Listen to their advice. Sometimes jobs are passed from one student to another by word of mouth.

Taught modules or courses

As part of the application process, you will probably have applied to study a set number of modules or courses. Different universities have different administration arrangements so you may find that you are preregistered on these courses or you may have to register on arrival. It is essential that you are registered on the correct modules or courses as these make up your formal degree programme. If you have any queries talk to people in your host and home institution. Normally you will not be allowed to change modules or courses without good reason and you will need to gain approval from your programme leader in your home institution.

Different institutions have different ways of organizing their taught modules or courses. In some institutions, you will be provided with a set timetable. In others you will be able to choose when you attend your modules or courses, as the same course may be repeated several times a week. This means that you will be able to organize your timetable yourself and sign up for courses at a time and place that suits you. Your tutor will be able to advice you on how your programme will be scheduled before you leave your own country. Alternatively, this is one of the important topics that will be covered during induction.

It is really important that you know who your contact person is in your host institution and liase with them and your tutor in your home institution if you have any problems or concerns with your studies.

Study culture

Different countries have different study cultures and you will need to adapt quickly to the new culture. Differences in study culture relate to whether or not the underlying approach to learning and teaching is tutor centred or student centred (see Chapter 4). If you attend a university or business school where the teaching approach is very tutor centred you are likely to find that you attend lots of lectures and that the whole approach to learning and teaching is prescribed. In contrast, if you attend a school or department where the approach is student centred you will be expected to work independently and take part in activities such as case studies, action learning, problem based learning. Many business schools and departments provide a mixture of tutor centred and student centred courses or modules. It is worthwhile being aware of these differences so that if you experience a very different study culture to your own you will allow yourself the time to adapt to the new culture. Reading Chapter 4 will help you to understand different approaches to learning and teaching.

Two contrasting study cultures are found in the USA and UK. In the USA the study culture involves regular homework which you are expected to complete and this is likely to involve reading a compulsory textbook and, at a later date, answering very specific test questions. You will experience frequent tests (often multiple choice tests) and these are often given without any advance warning. In addition, you will find that you are not expected to write long essays or projects, or to read extensively around your subject. You may find that marks are awarded for attendance at lectures and seminars, as well as contributions in class. This is quite different to the situation in the UK where the study culture involves relatively small numbers of timetabled classes and you are expected to work independently throughout the year. Your independent work will involve you preparing for classes and also researching and writing long essays, reports or dissertations. In addition, all tests are scheduled well in advance to give you time to prepare for them. Marks are sometimes awarded for attendance and contributions in seminars and workshops but this practice is not widespread.

Another difference in study culture relates to assessment practices and marking regimes. Different countries and different institutions have different practices.

This topic is considered in Chapter 6. If you are unclear about the assessment practices in your host institution then ask your tutors for advice.

The number of scheduled classes that you have will vary from country to country. In the UK students have a relatively small number of scheduled classes each week but they are expected to carry out substantial amounts of independent study. In contrast, in other European countries students are expected to attend many more scheduled classes but to do less independent research. When you start your study abroad period then your host institution is likely to make their study expectations clear during the induction period. It is worthwhile talking to home students at your host institution and finding out from them how they tackle the study culture in their country. However, ask a few people's opinions so that you can identify common practices.

The more you know about your host country and study culture then the easier it will be for you to adapt to your new situation. Before you leave your own country read up as much as possible about your host country and study culture. Read the websites of your host institution as this will provide you with useful information. Your tutors, in both your home and host institution, are likely to be very experienced in helping students to make the transition from one study culture to another. Do talk to them if you are finding it hard to adapt to the new learning culture or if you want specific advice. In addition, talk to students who have returned from their study abroad experience as they will be able to provide you with an insight into the study culture in your host country. Many business schools and departments organize social networking sites so that different groups of students can exchange experiences with each other.

In your host institution, you will find that you are able to bring your own cultural experiences to classroom discussions. Many lecturers enjoy teaching classes of international students and helping individuals from many different cultures bring their experiences into discussions. If asked, do be willing to share your experiences and perceptions with the whole class. This helps to enrich the learning experiences of everyone and it provides an important element of international business and management education. Sharing each other's cultural perceptions is a good basis for learning about intercultural working which is the basis of working in global businesses.

Computers

You will be provided with advice about whether or not you need to bring your own computer to your host institution. In addition, you will be given guidance about the availability of computer rooms and Internet access. The majority of institutions do provide computer rooms where students can access the computer facilities, but these resources may be limited both in terms of the numbers of available computers and the opening hours. Some student accommodation will provide Internet access while others will not. In general, most students take their own laptop with them when they study abroad. They often find that it is normal practice to take a laptop into the lecture or seminar and use it for making notes or finding relevant information from the Internet.

Money matters

In an earlier section in this chapter, you were provided with advice on the costs that you need to take into account for your study abroad experience. The day to day cost of living varies from country to country and you will need to budget for your living expenses. Again, your university or college will be able to provide you with advice and guidance.

In many countries you will need to set up a local bank account and you will be advised how to do this at induction. Credit cards are very useful, for example to book train tickets. Some students use their credit card all the time and use their bank account in their home country to pay the bill each month. In addition, a credit or debit card may be used to withdraw money via cashpoint machines. However, in some countries credit cards are not widely accepted.

You will find that your host institution provides a range of options for food. These are likely to include: self-catering, a meal plan where you pay for so many meals per week in the university or in student accommodation, or a combined accommodation and food contract. In general, if you pay in advance this is cheaper than paying for your food on a daily or weekly basis. However, it is well worth obtaining advice from returning students, obtaining information at induction and asking continuing students in your host institution before you make your final decision. Once you have signed up to a particular food option it may be difficult and expensive to change your mind. If you have special dietary requirements do check that they can be accommodated before you finalize your accommodation and food arrangements. If you have special dietary requirements and you are expected to stay with a host family this may cause difficulties. Your host family may not be equipped to provide a special diet and they may consider it rude that you are unwilling to eat their food. It is therefore important to discuss this issue with your department or business school *before* you finalize your arrangements.

Another item of expenditure is books and the cost of books varies from country to country. You will need to find out whether or not you are expected to buy books and also the type of library provision that you will have to support your studies. In some countries, you are expected to buy all your own textbooks and this may be very expensive. It is worth finding out about ways of buying secondhand books (e.g., over the Internet) or sharing textbooks. Again, returning students may be able to help you by selling their textbooks to you.

It is worth budgeting for trips around your host country. There are many very good travel deals available either by booking well ahead or by making the most of last minute deals. In addition, you may be able to use student or young people's travel offers. If you want to travel in a group with new friends there are sometimes very economical group deals for students.

Employment

Some students obtain employment either during or at the end of their study abroad period. You will need to check whether or not your visa allows you to work and whether you need a social security number. In some countries your visa will only permit you to work on-campus (i.e., at your host institution) and jobs vary but may include telesales, kitchen work, waitressing, cleaning, library work or sports related jobs. This is another topic that is likely to be covered during your induction week. However, be aware that if you are working and earning money this will cut down your available study, travel and also socialising time.

Transport

Public transport varies from country to country. You will need to find out about the systems available in your host country. Train and long distance coach travel are often the cheapest options and you are likely to be able to obtain student discounts. If you are a car driver then it is advisable to take your licence with you. Some car drivers find it helpful to have a few driving lessons in their host country to learn the road rules and regulations.

Social life

Social life varies from country to country, and from institution to institution. You will need to find out about the social life in your host institution and you will start to find out about it at induction. Rules and attitudes relating to alcohol vary too. For example, in the USA the legal age to drink alcohol is 21 years and this means that social life on campus is very different to that in the UK. If you drink alcohol then it is very important to find out the rules relating to alcohol in your host country and to follow them. Otherwise you may end up with a jail sentence.

Identification

You will need to find out whether or not you need to carry some form of identification (ID) with you and, in some countries, these are regularly checked. Again, different countries have different rules. Again, this topic is likely to be covered at induction.

Culture

When you go to a new country then you are likely to experience some level of 'culture shock', as you will be living and studying in a different culture. Culture shock arises as you become immersed in a culture which is different to your own, where the language, customs and ways of doing things may be different to your own. There may be a different approach to time spent studying and socialising. Food is likely to be different to that in your home country. Meals may be held at different times to those that you are accustomed to. Most people, even seasoned travellers, experience culture shock. If you experience culture shock you may feel anxious, confused or lost. You may experience mood swings. You may not be able to make sense of what is happening and you may miss out on important information or activities. The following tips should help you cope with culture shock:

- Be prepared. Attend all your briefing sessions in your home institution. Talk to returning students who will have experienced culture shock when they arrived at their host institution. Find out as much as possible about the study abroad experience before you set off
- Attend all induction sessions. Identify key people who will act as information sources and give you advice
- Socialize and make friends both with other international students and with home students. Talk about how you feel and ask for help. It is highly probable that other international students will be feeling the same as you do
- Watch and listen. Use this as an approach to understanding your new experiences
- Be open minded and try not to evaluate or judge other people. You will come across many different ways of living and studying. Talk to people and try to understand them and their ways of living and studying. This will help you to develop a sense of living in a culturally diverse world. Try not to compare everything to your own culture. The more open minded you are and the more interested you are in other people and their cultures the more you will gain from your study abroad experience
- You will have lots of different opportunities to participate in different activities and events. These all provide you with opportunities to network and make new friends. They will also help you to learn about different cultures
- Expect to feel anxious at times. It is normal to feel anxious if you are living and studying in a new culture. These feelings will go away as you become more familiar with your new situation. Acknowledge your feelings and talk to your friends about them.

Obeying the law

When you are living and studying in a different country you must obey the law of that country. Ignorance of the law is not accepted as an excuse in a court of law. This means that you need to behave in a sensible and sensitive way throughout your study abroad experience. You will be informed of major differences in the law during briefing sessions in your own country and also during induction. You will also be able to obtain relevant information from the Internet and from tourist guides.

A minority of students think that because they are studying abroad and a long way from their home and home institutions that they can behave in a way that is unacceptable in their home country (e.g., drinking too much, breaking traffic regulations, attempting to travel on a train without a ticket). This type of behaviour is unacceptable in their host country too. Each year a small number of students are expelled from their host institution as they have not obeyed the law and they may then face a disciplinary hearing in their home institution. In extreme cases, they have their programme of studies terminated. In addition, information about this behaviour is likely to be included in references to future employers as it casts doubt on the ability of the student to work in the world of business and management in a professional and ethical manner.

Assessing the professional or study abroad experiences

This is a relatively short but important section. Many professional placement or study abroad experiences count towards your final degree results. This means that you may be required to carry out a piece of assessed work based on your experiences.

It is important to start preparing for this assessed work before you start your professional placement or study abroad experience and you will need to:

- Obtain detailed information about the assessment requirements including the assessment task and criteria. If you are completing assessment tasks in your host institution make sure that you understand what is expected of you. If you are in any doubt then ask your tutor(s) for advice
- If possible look at successful assignments from previous students
- Identify the kinds of information that you will need to collect during your professional placement or study abroad experience

- Identify how you will be able to access the library of your home and host institutions
- Identify the tutorial support available.

During your professional placement or study abroad experience make sure that you work on your assessment activity. Chapter 6 provides guidance on common assessment activities including reports, reflective learning journals and presentations. If you are on a study abroad experience make sure that you know whether your host or home institutions are responsible for assessing your work. You will then need to follow the assessment guidelines of that institution.

At the end of your professional placement or study abroad experience you will need to complete your assessed work and hand it in. Again, see Chapter 6 for guidance on assessed work.

Returning to your studies

When you have completed your professional placement or study abroad experience then you will return to your home institution and continue your studies. Many students find that they experience a kind of reverse culture shock as they return to their studies. Some students experience a sense of loss as they miss their new friends, the collegiality of their work placement or the adventure of living abroad. Other students find it frustrating that family, friends and students who have not had a professional experience placement or study abroad experience do not appear to be very interested in their experiences. In addition, most people find that they have changed during this experience and that they come back as different people with perhaps different goals and ambitions. Consequently, they may find it difficult to fit in and adapt to their return to study.

Many departments and business schools run debriefing sessions for returning students and these will give you an opportunity to share your experiences with likeminded people. You will also be given advice on how to cope with the reverse culture shock and settle back into your studies. Most people find that keeping in touch with their new friends via social networking sites and also weekend visits or shared holidays also help you to integrate your experiences into your everyday life.

Finally, it is worthwhile keeping a record of your professional placement or study abroad experience and including this in your personal portfolio (see Chapters 1, 3 and 4). This will help you to capitalize on your experiences in your *curriculum vitae* and in future job applications.

Summary

Both the professional placement or study abroad experience provide great opportunities for you to broaden your horizons, make new friends and develop your knowledge and experience. In many ways, they provide an opportunity for a gap year which is structured and tuned in to fit into your programme of study. Thousands of business and management students take part in professional placement or study abroad experiences each year and these experiences help to enrich the lives of individuals and also universities and colleges. The key to successfully participating in a professional placement or study abroad experience is to be prepared and participate as fully as possible in the experience. In general, students who take part in a professional experience placement or a study abroad experience find that this gives them an edge in the jobs market over students who have not had this type of experience.

10

Where do I go from here?

Introduction • Gaining employment • What do you want to do next?
• Searching for employment opportunities • Developing your career as a
reflective manager • Keeping in touch – professional networks • Further study
• Summary

Introduction

The aim of this chapter is to provide you with guidance on developing your career and moving into employment or graduate study. The topics covered in this chapter include: gaining employment, developing your career as a reflective manager, keeping in touch/networking and further study.

This chapter provides you with links to a free website that provides you with additional content relevant to your career development. Whenever you see the icon 🐝 this is an indicator that you will be able to access additional information and activities on the website: www.openup.co.uk/businesssuccess

Gaining employment

It is sensible to start thinking about gaining employment at the start of your studies, which will mean that you have time to develop the right kind of profile for your chosen career. This topic is covered in Chapter 3. The process of gaining employment is likely to involve the following stages:

- Working out what you want to do
- Searching for employment
- Applying for a job
- The selection process:
  - Interviews
  - Assessment centres
  - Psychometric testing
- Managing job offers.

What do you want to do next?

It is worth spending some time thinking about what you want to do next and discussing this with friends and family, tutors and the careers services. It is likely that your careers service will be able to provide you with specialist guidance and this may include access to psychometric testing and personal profile tools, which will help you to identify careers that will suit your particular strengths.

If you are unsure about what to do after your degree it is a really good idea to visit the careers service. Most university and college careers services provide a wide range of services and resources including:

- Careers advisors who will be able to provide you with one to one confidential help
- A library that contains information about searching for employment, employers, vacancies files, information about work placements, graduate trainee opportunities, careers directories and books, recruitment brochures and application forms
- Careers events such as:
  - Recruitment fairs
  - Employer events
  - Workshops, e.g., on writing a *curriculum vitae*; successful interviews
- Up to date information on:
  - Vacancies
  - Bulletins and notice boards
- Specialist website.

Make contact with your careers service as early as possible during your studies. Sign up to be kept up to date with careers information. Most universities and colleges provide careers services for their graduates for a few years after they have completed their degree – or for life!

On the website you will find material that will help you to identify your career goals. You may find it useful to read and work through these materials both at an early stage in your business and management degree and when you are close to graduating. Many students find that their career goals change as they gain experience in the subjects involved in business and management, and also as they experience the world of work.

Searching for employment opportunities

There are many ways of obtaining employment, and sources of information about vacancies include:

- Internet
- Newspaper and magazine advertisements
- Specialist graduate vacancy publications, e.g., *Prospects Directory*, *Prospects Today*
- Careers services
- Job centres
- Recruitment agencies
- Careers fairs
- Networking, e.g., attending professional meetings
- Friends and family.

Further information and weblinks are available on the free website.

Preparing your *curriculum vitae*

Many business and management students are prompted to prepare a *curriculum vitae* (CV) as one of the development activities during their degree. Preparing a CV is a time consuming activity but it is worth doing as it will help you to focus your thoughts about gaining employment and it is an essential tool for job seekers.

Your CV will act as a 'brochure' that summarizes your career and allows employers to know your key skills, attributes and achievements. You should use it to sell yourself, obtain an interview and get yourself a job. Many organizations ask job applicants to send in a CV with an accompanying letter. They will then choose people to interview from the CVs. This means that your letter and CV should help them answer key questions:

- Can this person do the job?
- Is this the sort of person we are looking for?
- Why does this person want the job?

While you may spend three to six hours preparing your CV, prospective employers will spend less than a minute reading your CV. This means that your CV must:

- Present key information on the first page
- Be visually attractive
- Be easy to read.

It is worthwhile preparing a standard CV and then rewriting it and refocusing it for every application. Keep a track of which version of your CV you send to each employer – it is easy to become confused if you are sending out lots of applications.

Your CV should contain the following information:

- Personal details – name, address, phone number, email address. You do not need to include information about your age or marital status
- Education – qualifications, dates, name of school/college/university. Put your most recent and important qualifications first. Present lower level qualifications (e.g., GCSEs) in a list format so that they do not take up much space
- Employment – give job title, company name, dates. Highlight achievements and responsibilities. Focus on experience relevant to the job you are applying for. If you have had lots of part time work that is not relevant to the application then summarize each briefly
- Additional experience/achievements – include those that strengthen your case
- Interests – select them carefully. Avoid mentioning any interests that might put off an employer. Don't overstate your interests – you may be required to talk about them.

Further information about CVs including the differences between a skills based CV and a traditional CV is available on the website.

When you produce your CV look at examples provided by your careers service and also compare your draft CV with those of your friends. This will help you to identify ways of improving it. Important points to remember when producing your CV include:

- Make it short (no more than two sides of A4)
- Make it quick and easy to read
- Use a clear and simple layout
- Present key information first
- Use reverse chronological order (most recent first)
- Include education, skills, training
- Include work experience (paid and unpaid)
- Include voluntary work
- Include other achievements and experiences
- Include personal details (name, address, phone number).

Remember that an employer is likely to spend less than a minute looking at your CV and this means that you need to make a good first impression. Discarded CVs often have the following problems:

- Spelling or grammatical errors
- Typographical errors
- Too much or too little information
- Irrelevant information
- Jokes or sarcastic comments
- Inappropriate comments.

Example CVs are included on the website.

Application forms

Many employers do not accept CVs and want you to complete an application form instead, as this will provide them with specific information that they wish to use to assess your suitability for their vacancy.

Further advice on completing application forms is available on the free website.

Covering letters

Many employers request a covering letter with your CV or application form. The covering letter is as important as your CV (or application form) and the employer will use it as part of the shortlisting process. You will find it helpful to use the letter to highlight special skills and experience that are relevant to the particular job. Type the letter (unless you are asked for a handwritten letter) and use white paper.

Further information about covering letters including common errors and also example letters are provided in the website.

Interviews

If you are invited for an interview then it important to read the information provided by your potential employer and follow all the instructions. Preparing for your interview is likely to involve the following activities:

- Research the company. Use the business information unit in your public library, your university library, the Internet and other information sources to find out as much as possible about the company
- Read all the information that has been sent to you. Make notes so that you are clear about the type of person they are looking for (see the person specification) and the job (read the job description)
- Prepare for the interview by working through the types of questions that might be asked. See the sample list of questions on the website
- Work out positive answers to the questions and make sure that all your answers relate to this particular company, job description and person specification
- Ask a friend to give you a mock interview. Listen to their feedback
- Work out what you will wear for the interview. Think about the culture of the organization and the likely dress code. If in doubt, dress formally rather than informally
- Work out your travel arrangements. Allow plenty of time for delays
- Get a good night's sleep the night before the interview.

Most interviews are divided into three parts:

1 Beginning
   - Welcome
   - Introductions
     ○ Name, role
     ○ Shake hands
   - Creating rapport
     ○ Talk about niceties, weather, travel, etc.
   - Explanation of the interview procedure
   - Summarizing the job

2 Middle
  • A series of preprepared questions
  • Each question may be followed up by additional supplementary questions or discussion
  • One or more people are likely to make notes of the responses
3 End
  • Opportunity for you to ask questions
  • Explanation about travel expenses, other details
  • Explanation of how you will be informed of the results of the interview
  • Thank you and goodbyes.

Further information about interviews including commonly asked questions is available on the website.

Assessment centres

Many organizations use assessment centres as part of their recruitment and selection process. Typically candidates will be asked to attend the assessment centre for one to three days. During this time they may take part in team activities, individual activities and social activities.

  Preparing for your visit to the assessment centre involves the following:

  • Reading all the instructions
  • Finding out about the organization
  • Finding out more about assessment centres, e.g., by visiting your careers service
  • Practicing aptitude tests (your careers service will be able to provide you with sample tests)
  • Practicing specialist tests, e.g., IT tests, numeracy tests, English tests
  • Making sure that you arrive at the assessment centre on time and dressed in a professional manner.

At the assessment centre, you may be involved in the following types of activities:

  • Team activities
    ○ Discussions
    ○ Teamwork activities
    ○ Role play
  • Individual activities

- ○ Business simulation
- ○ Written tests
- ○ Numerical tests
- ○ Presentation
- ○ Interviews
- ○ Psychometric tests
- Social and other activities
  - ○ Formal meal
  - ○ Sports activities
  - ○ Presentations by company.

Further guidance on typical assessment centre activities is available in the website.

Developing your career as a reflective manager

Chapter 3 provides guidance on becoming a reflective student and developing reflective practice as a means of helping you to be successful in your studies. Reflective practice is equally important in the workplace and it is a way in which you can improve your knowledge and skills on a day to day basis.

During your time as a student, you may have developed your portfolio or e-portfolio and it is a good idea to continue this or start a new one as you go into the workplace. If you have not maintained a portfolio you may find that your new employer requires you to keep one. Personal portfolios or continuous professional development (CPD) portfolios are a common feature in the workplace.

Further guidance on workplace portfolios is available on the website.

Another approach to becoming a reflective manager is to work with a mentor. Mentoring involves spending time (face to face, on the phone or by email) with a more experienced manager, and it is an important way of gaining support in the following areas:

- Moving from one role to another
- Dealing with a specific issue or problem

- Skills for a particular task or project
- Training support and development
- Professional contacts and networks
- Career and professional development.

Essentially a mentor is a friend and someone who will support your personal and career development. Some organizations have formal mentoring schemes, and these are typically aimed at new recruits and/or groups of staff who traditionally find barriers to their progression (e.g., women or people from ethnic minorities). Informal mentoring schemes are very common and may be initiated by the mentee, their line manager or a colleague. Typically individuals may identify a mentor within their own organization, but some workers (e.g., consultants) find it appropriate to approach a colleague in another organization. Some universities and colleges offer mentoring schemes for new graduates, for example they may be matched up with an experienced manager who may be an alumni.

As a new or recent graduate it is well worth considering and possibly setting up a supportive mentoring process for yourself. Think about who may be able to act as your mentor and what you want to gain from the mentoring relationship. Some people work with more than one mentor, for example a recent graduate carrying out market research and working on a new website project may work with two mentors, one for each aspect of their work. Typically, mentoring involves meeting up with your mentor (e.g., at three monthly intervals) and exploring your current situation and career plan. If you are seeking someone to mentor you as you progress from one role or project to another it is important to choose someone with experience of that type of work and who keeps up to date with new ideas and professional developments.

Further information about mentors and mentoring is available on the website.

Keeping in touch – professional networks

People working within a particular profession (e.g., accountancy, economics, human resource management or marketing) keep in touch with each other by becoming involved in local, regional, national or international networks. Many of these networks are established and maintained by professional associations such as the Chartered Institute for Personnel and Development (CIPD) or the Chartered Management Institute (CMI).

Professional associations are important as they provide a means of becoming a chartered practitioner, in other words they manage the professional development and quality assurance of new members to the profession. This means that if you wish to become chartered (e.g., a chartered accountant or human resource manager) you will need to join the association and take part in the required professional development activities. Once you have met their requirements you will receive the relevant professional qualification. Membership fees vary and are often linked with salaries. However, the benefits of membership includes access to professional journals, access to specialist networks and groups, and, often, discounted fees for professional indemnity insurance, training events or books.

Some professional associations have their own information service and will provide detailed advice and guidance over the phone or by email. Support, advice, training and development can be obtained through attending workshops and other training events. These are often offered at the headquarters of professional associations as well as at venues around the country. In addition, many local and specialist groups offer their own training events and these are often relatively cheap to attend, without the expense of travel costs. Professional conferences are also a good way of developing a network and although they often have the advantage of being located in beautiful venues they do require hard work if you are to get the most out of them. Effective participation in conferences requires individuals to be assertive, make contacts and spend time getting to know colleagues. One of the best ways of achieving this is to become actively involved in a specialist group and to volunteer to go on their committee and so move into the centre of professional activities.

Nowadays, many professional activities take place through online communication tools such as discussion and mailing lists. Discussion lists can be used in a variety of ways and, in general, they provide a forum for:

- Requesting factual information
- Requesting advice and opinions or experiences
- Information about new websites, products, publications
- Advice on buying or using new systems or products
- Conference and meeting announcements
- Staff development announcements
- Information about vacancies.

The advantages of becoming involved in a professional association, even if it does not lead to a professional qualification are huge. It will enable you to network and become known within your profession. This in turn is likely to mean that you will have access to information about job vacancies and organizations that are not publicised through the normal channels of the press or Internet.

In addition to professional networks, you will also be able to join the networks established by your own university or college (i.e., the alumni networks). Again, this is an important source of information and help. Many business schools have alumni networks around the world and these organize meetings and other events for their members. If you are travelling to or working in one of these countries it provides a relatively easy route into the professional networks of the country. The alumni office of the university or college will be able to provide you with help and guidance.

Additional information about professional networks is available on the website.

Further study

Many students now enhance their careers by postgraduate study either in the subject of their first degree or in a new subject. If you are interested in postgraduate study then it is worthwhile finding out what is available. There is a wide range of postgraduate qualifications including:

- Master of Law (LLM)
- Master of Research (MRes)
- Master of Philosophy (MPhil)
- Master of Science (MSc)
- Master of Arts (MA)
- Master of Business Administation (MBA)
- Postgraduate Certificate in Education (PGCE)
- Postgraduate Diploma (PgDip)
- Doctor of Philosophy (PhD).

If you are thinking about doing further study it is a good idea to think about whether you want to focus on:

- Academic research
- Developing subject knowledge
- Gaining a vocational qualification.

If you are interested in academic research and a potential career as an academic in a university, it is normal practice to gain a PhD or DPhil in your chosen subject. If you are interested in this career path then a good starting point is to talk to lecturers in your department or business school. The university careers service and graduate school will also be able to provide you with help and support.

Many students decide that they want to follow up a subject through a taught graduate study. Typically they may choose an MSc or MA programme in their chosen subject and the basic entrance requirement for these programmes is a 2:1 or 1st class degree. In the UK, these programmes involve two semesters of taught modules followed by a period of independent study as you complete the dissertation. Many students continue with their graduate studies at the university or college of their first degree. However, there are advantages to be gained from moving to a different institution, as this will broaden your perspectives and provide new ways of looking at your subject. Some postgraduate programmes (e.g., the MBA) are designed for individuals with managerial experience rather than new graduates.

Many students want to top up their first degree with a postgraduate qualification (e.g., in law, accountancy, education, IT or librarianship). If this is the case then you will need to carry out research and apply for a place. Your careers service will be able to provide you with information and advice. Competition is normally very high for places on vocational programmes so it is sensible to apply as early as possible, for example at the start of your final year.

Funding for postgraduate study varies depending on the programme and the institution offering it. In addition, there are sometimes special grants (e.g., from the government or European Union funds) or 'golden handshakes' available in shortage subjects. Other funding options include: career development loans from a bank or other agency; university bursaries and scholarships; commercial sponsorship; charities and trusts. Again, use the resources of your careers service to help you track down the information you need.

Further information about postgraduate study is available on the website.

Summary

This chapter provides you with guidance on developing your career and moving into employment or graduate study. It is a relatively short chapter as additional information and activities are provided in the associated free website at: www.openup.co.uk/businesssuccess

This chapter provides advice on gaining employment and covers topics such as writing your CV, application forms, interviews and assessment centres. Once you have obtained your first graduate post it is important to take charge of your professional development, which involves becoming a reflective manager and maintaining your professional portfolio. You can enhance your career opportunities by taking part in professional networks and by gaining the support of a mentor. Finally, while some students say 'never again' when they get to the end of their first degree, others find that they want to return to study and the final section in this chapter outlines these postgraduate study routes.

The main message in this book is that the skills required for successfully completing a business or management degree are also those that will also enable you to be successful in the workplace and your chosen career. Students who take full advantage of the opportunities offered by student life are those who are often the best equipped for working in local or global organizations and in dealing with complexity and uncertainty.

References

Allan, B. (2006) *Supervising and Leading Teams*. London: Facet Publishing.

Allan, B. (2007) *Blended Learning*. London: Facet Publishing.

Boud, D. J., Keogh, R. and Walker, D. (eds) (1985) *Reflection: Turning Experience into Learning*. London: Kogan Page.

Bryman, A. and Bell, E. (2007) *Business Research Methods*. Oxford: Oxford University Press.

Cameron, S. (2005) *Business Student's Handbook*, 2nd edn. Harlow: Prentice Hall.

Cottrell, S. (1999) *The Study Skills Handbook*. London: Macmillan.

Dunn, R. and Dunn, K. (1999) *The Complete Guide to Learning Styles*. Boston, MA: Allyn and Bacon.

Entwistle, N. (1981) *Styles of Learning and Meaning*. New York: John Wiley.

Goleman, D. (1995) *Emotional Intelligence*. London: Bloomsbury.

Honey, P. and Mumford, A. (1992) *The Manual of Learning Styles*. Maidenhead: Peter Honey.

Kahn, P. and O'Rourke, K. (2005) *Understanding Enquiry-based Learning*, http://www.aishe.org/readings/2005-2/contents.html (accessed 12 May 2007).

Kolb, D. A. (1984) *Experiential Learning: Experience as the Source of Learning and Development*. Englewood Cliffs, NJ: Prentice-Hall.

Moon, J. (2000) *Reflection in Learning and Professional Development*. London: Kogan Page.

Pedler, M., Burgoyne, J. and Boydell, T. (2001) *A Manager's Guide to Self Development*, 4th edn. London: McGraw-Hill.

Radnor, H. (2001) *Researching your Professional Practice: Doing Interpretive Research*. Buckingham: Open University Press.

Revans, R. W. (1980) *The ABC of Action Learning*. Bromley: Chartwell-Bratt.

Salmon, G. (2000) *E-moderating*. London: Kogan Page.

Savin-Baden, M. (2006) *Problem-based Learning Online*. Buckingham: Open University Press.

Wellington, J. *et al.* (2005) *Succeeding with your Doctorate*. London: Sage.

Index